D0980030

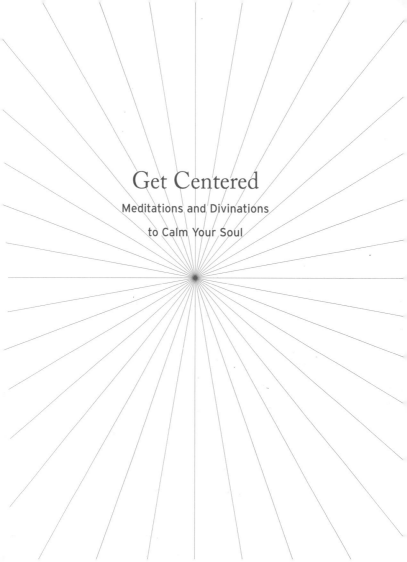

Get Centered

Meditations and Divinations
to Calm Your Soul

Get Centered

گیگ سینترد

متمرکز   تمکز، عبادت، ہاندیشہ، خیال، ہمراقبہ

مدیتیشن   دونیشن

Meditations and Divinations

مال سی، حدس درست   تأملات ویشن کور

تعبیر رویا، ہمال، فال =

سول

to Calm Your Soul

کاٹم   برای آرامش روح خو

روح-ضمیر   آرام-سلامت-سکان-ملایم

خاطرجو   آسودہ-بی سروصدائی

By Nathaniel Altman and

Sirona Knight

△

Sterling Publishing Co., Inc.
New York

Library of Congress Cataloging-in-Publication Data available on request.

Material in this collection was adapted from:
The Little Giant Encyclopedia of Meditations & Blessings
© 2000 by Nathaniel Altman
The Little Giant Encyclopedia of Runes
© 2000 by Sirona Knight

10 9 8 7 6 5 4 3 2 1

Published by Sterling Publishing Co., Inc.
387 Park Avenue South, New York, NY 10016
© 2005 by Sterling Publishing Co. Inc.
Distributed in Canada by Sterling Publishing Co., Inc.
c/o Canadian Manda Group, 165 Dufferin Street,
Toronto, Ontario, Canada M6K 3H6
Distributed in the United Kingdom by GMC Distribution Services
Castle Place, 166 High Street, Lewes, East Sussex, England BN7 1XU
Distributed in Australia by Capricorn Link (Australia) Pty. Ltd.
P.O. Box 704, Windsor, NSW 2756, Australia

ISBN-13: 978-1-4027-2945-4
ISBN-10: 1-4027-2945-6

For information about custom editions, special sales,
premium and corporate purchases, please contact Sterling Special Sales
Department at 800-805-5489 or specialsales@sterlingpub.com.

Contents

Introduction

Meditation is a powerful tool that provides a multitude of benefits. In addition to providing relaxation and calm, meditation has been used throughout history to help people on the often difficult paths of integration and healing. Evidence gleaned from hundreds of controlled medical trials has shown that meditation can greatly enhance the body's innate ability to heal itself of a wide range of diseases. By practicing meditation-even if only a few minutes a day-we can enhance our lives in a powerful and lasting way. Not only can it help us to enjoy a more fulfilling life, but can have a great impact on the lives of those around us.

You will find here many different types of meditation techniques drawn from a wide variety of spiritual traditions, including guided meditations, meditating on sacred symbols,

meditating to music, chanting, Zazen meditation, walking meditations, meditation in nature, writing meditations, Tantric meditation, and healing meditations.

There is also a section on meditations with runes–powerful symbols linked to Norse mythology. Runes are universal and nondenominational, so anyone can use them. They serve as a direct symbol-language to connect the conscious and the unconscious, helping you tap into archetypal images, ancestral memories, and the creative source, accessing your innermost feelings and intuitions. This makes them ideal meditation tools for use in spiritual growth and psychological integration.

While you may be primarily drawn to meditations that reflect your own religious beliefs, you might also consider the offerings of other religious traditions as well, if only to gain a deeper understanding and appreciation of the spiritual beliefs of other members of the human family. There are treasures to be found throughout the spectrum of religious diversity.

Use this book as a tool to develop your own meditation practice to open yourself to a higher power, as well as to spiritual power within you, and link yourself more strongly to those around you. Consult this book at any time to relax, expand your consciousness, and enjoy your life to its fullest.

Chapter One:
Why and How to Meditate

Mindful Awareness

Today's world seems to be moving faster and faster. Despite labor-saving devices we seem to work longer hours than ever before. Many of us find it difficult to balance work, quality time with our family, and precious time by ourselves. We are increasingly bombarded by information, opinions, and hype from the media, advertising, and the Internet. In an age of material abundance, many of us are unhappy-we want "something more" in our lives.

Meditation provides a way to help us see the outer world-and ourselves-more clearly. It can also help us learn to relate to our family, friends, and coworkers in a deeper, more meaningful way.

Meditation has been called "mindful awareness": consciousness of both the world around us and our own inner world, with its drama, conflicts, and fears. It also brings awareness of the calm, intelligent, inner essence that some religions call "the soul."

An increasing amount of research has been done that reveals the many benefits of meditation. On a purely physical level, regular meditation practice has been found to:

* Lower blood pressure
* Reduce anxiety and stress
* Improve immune system function
* Increase energy and stamina
* Help manage asthma flare-ups and other allergic reactions
* Help manage pain

Many meditators have reported such lasting mental and psychological benefits as:

* Increased ability to be calm
* Improved mental focus
* Expanded perspectives
* Greater empathy and compassion for others
* Enhanced creativity
* Improved memory
* Improved sleep

* Deeper contact with their spiritual essence
* Reduced use/interest in drugs and alcohol
* Greater feelings of optimism
* Greater efficiency at work and school
* A clearer sense of their personal goals

Lower Self, Higher Self

The human mind is a complex and amazing thing. Humans have the ability to live in different states of reality, which can vary tremendously. On one hand, we a have a childlike side that is often vain, selfish, opinionated, and destructive. Its time frame is confined to the here and now, not unlike a spoiled (but likeable) child whose needs demand his or her parents' immediate attention. While this part of ourselves may get us into trouble, it also makes our lives very interesting! Spiritual teachers have called this part the "lower self" that looks out for its own interests and wants its own way at any cost.

We also have another side that is known variously as the "universal self," the "higher self," or the "spark of God within." More quiet and subtle than the lower self, it possesses superior wisdom, love, and strength that are inclusive, compassionate, and ageless. Sometimes we are lucky enough to know an older, insightful person who is a source of common sense, practical wisdom, and infinite patience. This person accepts us the way we are without judgment, and is happy to offer counsel that is always insightful and helpful. Such an elder is a source of calm and stability in an often crazy world.

The higher self is not unlike that discerning person. No matter what time of day or night, or wherever we happen to be, we can go to that special someone for comfort, wisdom, and inspiration.

In addition to the higher and lower self, we also possess the knowledge and will of the mind. When it comes to meditation, this part is very important. To be in touch with our will and sense of knowledge can help us achieve several important goals:

1. It allows us to observe how our childlike destructive side lives through attitudes, ideas, fears, emotions, and activities that cause us conflicts, keep us separate from others, undermine our happiness, and prevent us from being integrated and whole human beings.

2. At the same time, it can open us to the universal, unlimited part of our beings. This not only allows us to contact deeper realities, but also enables us to confront and eventually transform negative currents that make us anxious, fearful, angry, and generally unhappy.

3. Rather than make us holy, meditation helps us realize that we are already holy: It enables us to see more clearly who we already are.

Meditation: The Key

A spiritual teacher wrote that we create our own reality by the sum total of our feelings, our conscious (and subconscious) opinions, and our personal attitudes and goals. Taken together, these thoughts, attitudes, and emotions determine our actions in daily life, as well as our reactions to what is going on around us. According to a booklet published by the Meditation Group for the New Age in Ojai, California:

> *Every human action is the result of some inner activity. All too often it is our desires and uncontrolled thoughts which drive us, and this can bring about all sorts of difficulties and even have harmful consequences, both for the individual and for mankind in general. This is why it is essential to become the masters of our own inner realm, creating in this subjective world only what we consider to be right and constructive and contributing to the common good on these inner planes as much as we would in the outer world.*

Many of us experience our inner life as a tangled mass of contradictory thoughts and feelings. We often indulge in fear and negative thinking, which causes us anxiety and pain. Most of us are the source of literally hundreds of negative thoughts, angry emotions, and hurtful attitudes every single day.

By dedicating ourselves to challenging wrong ideas, letting go of unhelpful emotional patterns, and dealing with destructive feelings in a spirit of honesty and courage, we not only create a new life for ourselves, but benefit every living being on Earth. Meditation is the key that begins this magical process.

A Creative Process

Meditation is considered a creative process. Since our attitudes, feelings, and beliefs are constantly manifesting themselves every single day, our most important task is to become aware of what we think, how we feel, and what we believe. Though it's not always comfortable, we especially need to become aware of those negative thoughts and feelings that are hidden from view, because their power is greatest when we don't know (or merely suspect) that they are there.

At the same time, we need to acknowledge and honor our positive thoughts and feelings and allow them fuller expression. Like a gardener who nurtures a tiny acorn until it is able to grow into a powerful oak tree, we need to nurture our positive thoughts and feelings until they become a dominant aspect of our nature.

Whenever we focus on what is going on inside and observe our inner landscape in greater detail, our awareness of who we really are is strengthened. We also contact what teachers call "the infinite self," which helps us become more integrated and whole. When our inner awareness is strengthened, we are able to transform negative attitudes and destructive emotions, and limit our beliefs to positive qualities that bring more excitement, integration, and happiness into our lives. According to the spiritual teacher H. Saraydarian:

Thus meditation must be handled as a part of our daily life. In all our activity, expression, and relationships, meditation has to be present, not as an object by itself, but as a vital factor in all undertakings.

As with any other skill, meditation works best when practiced daily. Over time, we become more able to tap into the wellspring of unlimited love and wisdom that promotes inner healing and harmony in all of our relationships and activities. Simply stated, meditation can help us create a new life.

Rules of the Road for Prospective Meditators

Just as water is essential for our physical well-being, meditation is essential for our mental and spiritual well-being. Yet if we drink water too quickly, or consume water in excess, it can be harmful to our health. By the same token, we can only derive maximum benefit from meditation if it is practiced appropriately and with care. Although all the meditations here are safe when practiced correctly, advice will be given to assure success with each method. Most are geared more for beginners, while others are appropriate for advanced meditators.

1. The desire to meditate should come from good intentions, not from seeking mental, emotional, or psychic power to wield over others. Psychic power evolves naturally through self-awareness and selfless service.

2. Because meditation challenges old emotional and mental patterns, an open-minded attitude is essential. Otherwise, meditation can actually reinforce negative habits.

3. If meditation practice is too intense over a long period of time, insomnia, irritability, and emotional instability can result. This can be due to excessive breathing exercises, meditation sessions that are too long, or the overuse of mantras.

4. The insights gained through meditation need to be real. Ask: How may this truth be expressed in my everyday life?

5. Meditation can make us more aware of our faults. We need to avoid indulging in negative self-judgments and focus instead on acknowledgment and transformation.

6. Meditation is not recommended for young children, and only for teenagers who genuinely feel attracted to it. However, relaxation exercises, simple breathing exercises, hatha yoga, and T'ai Chi help young people to become centered and "grounded."

7. Do not meditate (or stop meditating) if you:
* Feel tired
* Feel nervous
* Are having digestive problems
* Have a headache

* Have taken drugs or alcohol
* Feel aggressive or critical toward others
* Are becoming forgetful
* Feel that you are being forced to meditate

Practical Meditation: Foundations

Seasoned meditators teach that there are four basic "pillars" that can help support our daily meditation practice. By building them for ourselves, we can greatly enhance our meditation experience. They are:

* Creating a sacred environment
* Choosing an appropriate meditation posture
* Learning how to relax
* Learning how to breathe

1. Creating Sacred Space

Although one can meditate anywhere at any time of the day or night, those of us who have the opportunity to meditate at home can create an environment that will help us get the most out of this practice.

First, find a place that is quiet and has good ventilation. Some can devote an entire room to meditation, using it exclusively for that purpose. Decorating this room with a thick carpet, white or light-colored walls, and a simple straight-backed chair or meditation cushions or mats, will help create a comfortable environment conducive to meditation. You may also wish to place sacred objects in the room, such as portraits of spiritual teachers, a symbol such as a cross or Jewish star, a statue or drawing of the Buddha or other religious item. Many people also include fresh flowers and crystals. The idea is to create a space that will uplift your spirits—a personal sanctuary apart from the workaday world.

If you do not have the space to create a meditation room, the next best choice is to use a study, a den, or another room where you can be apart from the rest of the household for thirty minutes at a time.

Creating a Home Altar Creating an altar in your home is a very personal undertaking. The altar exists to remind you of your inner life. It can also serve as a centerpiece for your meditation practice or a place where you say daily prayers.

You can create your altar on a small table, or even on a shelf, but it should be located where you can visit often and in private, away from the most frequented areas of your home. Decorating the altar depends on your personal taste, and should reflect what you want, rather than what you think is appropriate for an altar. The altar may have a simple cloth covering onto which you might place one or more votive candles, a religious symbol, a statue or picture of one or more saints or spiritual teachers, an incense holder, prayer beads, or crystals. Fresh flowers add to the beauty and spiritual presence of any home altar and should be replaced regularly.

Some people create an altar from empty space in a cluttered room, which sets it apart from the rest of the home. Whatever type of altar you choose to create, include only elements that are personally important to you.

As a sacred place in your home and a focal point to help you commune with the spiritual realms, your altar should always be kept clean and free from dirt, dust, or anything else that is not intended to be part of the altar.

In time, your altar can become a veritable "power spot" in your home. Like an electrical generator, it can be a repository of all of your feelings of devotion, compassion, and positive intent-a continual source of positive energy in your home for the benefit of all who reside or visit there.

Incense Incense has traditionally been used not only to eliminate odors, but to clean the subtle energies of a space. It is also believed to uplift the spirit. Some of the best incense is made at the headquarters of the Theosophical Society in Madras, India (available through Quest bookshops or Theosophical bookshops all over the world), and the Auroshikha Agarbathies incense made at the Sri Aurobindo Ashram in Pondicherry, India (available in many metaphysical bookstores). Usually, incense that comes from a spiritual center is made with more care and greater consciousness than incense made in an ordinary factory. In any case, it is always a good idea to bless the incense before using it, since it has probably been handled by many different people before you purchased it.

Many different types of incense are available, and you need to choose the type that is most compatible with your needs. If you are studying meditation with a teacher, he or she will be able to recommend a particular type that is best for you. If you are choosing your own incense, the following guide may be helpful:

Rose * opens your heart and awakens love.

Lavender * stimulates the yin and yang balance;
steadies and calms the emotions.

Jasmine * enhances self-image and promotes confidence.

Lotus * inspires the desire to meditate; it also helps develop
trust and receptivity in relationships.

Patchouli * awakens the desire for transformation;
helps increase your energy level.

Sandalwood * stimulates the intuitive senses;
awakens the desire to merge with the Divine within.

Frankincense * inspires spiritual recognition; elevates the mind
and the emotions.

Myrrh * strengthens endurance; helps preserve youthful
innocence.

Musk * stimulates your primal instincts and helps draw
a sexual partner. This incense may not be suitable for
spiritually oriented meditation.

Saffron * awakens us to the Joy of the Gods; it is sometimes

used in Tantra yoga and other forms of sexual ritual and
devotion.

Gardenia ✱ is believed to assist in opening the energy centers
or chakras.

Olive ✱ arouses passion and bonding; develops grounded
sensuality.

Almond ✱ helps rekindle an awareness of sexual mysteries.

Coconut ✱ arouses desire for the exotic and opens you to new
horizons; it is said to help bring out deep inner feeling.

As an alternative to incense, you can use aromatic oils to
eliminate room odors and cleanse the subtle atmosphere of a
room. Place several drops of mint, pine, or eucalyptus oil in
a glass of water and place the water near the place where you
practice meditation.

Creating an Outdoor Altar For those who have a quiet backyard, an
outdoor altar can be a source of serenity and strength during
the warmer months of the year, or all year-round if you live
in a warm or temperate climate.

The altar will, of course, vary according to your personal taste. Some erect a small religious statue surrounded by a
protective structure, while others prefer the statue or religious object to be exposed to the elements. The altar is often
surrounded by flowers and decorative shrubbery, such as
ornamental conifers or flowering plants, like roses.

A Tree Shrine In many cases, a tree on your property can become a tree shrine. Many of us instinctively feel that certain trees express a powerful energy with a special "keynote" quality, like protection, healing, wisdom, or inspiration. The emotional and spiritual links between a human and a tree shrine can be quite profound. If a person is sufficiently open and sensitive, just visiting a tree shrine can be a religious experience, which may assist in healing or personal transformation.

Selecting a tree to use as a tree shrine is a simple matter. If your property contains lots of trees, intuitively search out the tree towards which you feel the closest bond. Or you may decide to choose a tree because of its secluded location. In Thailand, Buddhist monks designate a sacred tree by tying an orange ribbon around its trunk. Some people attach religious items to the tree, such as a cross, a statue of the Buddha, or the image of a saint. The tree becomes a type of altar under which you can meditate and pray when the weather is good.

A tree shrine can be a friend for a lifetime. By developing a close relationship with a tree, we deepen our connection and love for the Earth, growing wiser and more sensitive to the life around us. We learn how to be more effective "Earth stewards" who assist in the protection and healing of our planetary home. A tree shrine does not have to be planted. Many are already there and merely have to be acknowledged.

Like the altar in your home, an outdoor altar or tree shrine should be kept clean and well maintained, and should not be used for purposes other than those related to your spiritual practice.

No Rushing The place that becomes your sacred meditation space will be the primary space (or one of the primary places) in which you will engage in meditation and prayer. After you meditate or pray, do not immediately get up and begin your daily tasks. Linger a few moments in receptive silence in the sacred space you have created. Follow this by quietly doing some simple tasks in a meditative spirit. This serves as a "living bridge" between your meditation practice and your more mundane daily life.

2. *Meditation Postures*

There are numerous postures that people use when they meditate. Some are better designed for Westerners than others. While a full lotus posture may be appropriate for an Indian saddhu or holy man, it may be extremely difficult (let alone uncomfortable) for a stressed-out executive who is exploring meditation for the first time. Some postures involve sitting on the floor or on a meditation mat, while others call for sitting in a straight-backed chair, or lying on a mat or on the floor.

Whichever posture you choose, the following general guidelines may be useful:

✳ Your back and neck need to be reasonably straight, resulting in what some meditators call a "dignified" posture.

* The inner organs (especially the stomach, lungs, and intestines) should be free from pressure. If your shirt and pants feel tight, release the top button. Some meditate in comfortable Indian-style clothing that skims the body loosely and does not bind the internal organs in any way. Others prefer to wear a jogging suit, or sweat pants and a T-shirt.

* During meditation, your blood should circulate unimpeded. If your legs fall asleep during meditation, the discomfort will disrupt your practice. It may also make it impossible to get up when you are finished!

Sitting on the Floor Some feel comfortable sitting cross-legged on a cushion or a mat. There are also special "meditation chairs" that support your back sold in metaphysical book and supply stores or the Internet. Many Westerners prefer a simple, straight-backed chair that is neither too Spartan nor overly comfortable. Attempting to meditate in an overstuffed lounge chair or on a comfortable sofa often leads to drowsiness or sleep.

Meditating in a Chair Sit with feet placed firmly on the floor, knees comfortably straight. This helps balance your body and keeps it free from tension.

Place your hands on your knees or thighs facing either up or down. You might also place your left hand on your lap facing up, and your right hand, also palm up, on top of it. With the palms up, you may also intertwine your fingers and place them on your lap. Another recommended hand position is to place your hands on your thighs, palms facing up, gently touching each thumb to the tip of the index or middle finger of the same hand.

The Half-Lotus The half-lotus posture involves sitting cross-legged on the floor or on a mat or cushion. Place your right foot gently on your left thigh. Be sure to keep your left foot on the floor under your right thigh. Reposition yourself until you're comfortable. Place your hands, palms up, on your thigh, either open or with your thumbs to the tips of index or middle fingers.

The Full Lotus As in the half-lotus, you sit on the floor, preferably on a meditation mat or thin cushion. Gently place your right foot on your left thigh and your left foot on your right thigh. Newcomers to meditation often find this position impossible to achieve, so don't feel badly if you have trouble with it. One of the goals in meditation is to feel comfortable. While your ability to achieve the full lotus posture may be an indicator of a flexible body, it is not necessarily a sign of advanced spirituality!

Kneeling In this posture, you kneel on the meditation cushion with feet together, and place your weight on your knees and feet.

Whatever posture you choose, be aware of it if your body or head leans forward or to the side. Gently correct your posture so that your spine is comfortably straight, head resting naturally.

More about Meditation Many people close their eyes during meditation. You can also close your mouth and breathe through your nose. Place the tip of your tongue gently on the roof of your mouth behind the front teeth. Fold your hands so that the tips of your thumbs touch, or rest the backs of your hands on your knees with thumb and forefinger touching.

Begin meditating for five to ten minutes, and gradually increase the length of your session over time to twenty or thirty minutes. Experienced meditators are able to remain in a posture for three hours or more.

When you rise after concluding your meditation, do so gently. If you feel stiffness or pain anywhere in your body, massage that area gently until it feels better. Get up slowly, with dignity.

3. Basic Relaxation Exercises

Before you begin any of the meditations described in this book, you may want to use one of these simple methods, or take elements from them that work for you.

I. Tension/Release Exercise This simple technique can also serve as a complete meditation in itself.

1. Sit in a comfortable position, either in a half-lotus posture on a cushion, or upright on a comfortable, straight-backed chair.

2. Be aware of your breathing, slow down your breathing rate gradually, taking deeper, more rhythmic breaths. When you exhale, say the word "peace" aloud, or use another word with peaceful connotations, such as shanti or shalom. A goal in breath rate would be a count of six as you inhale, and a count of six when you exhale.

3. Be aware of any tension in your body. Silently scan your face, neck, shoulders, chest, arms, hands, stomach, pelvis, legs, and feet to perceive any areas of tension.

4. If you come upon an area that is tense, direct your calming breath to that area. When you inhale, visualize the breath moving toward the tense area, and bathe it with warm, calming energy. As you exhale, visualize the tension leaving that part of your body. Continue this process until your body is completely relaxed.

II. Progressive Relaxation Exercise (1)

1. Sit comfortably in a straight-backed chair or cross-legged on a bed or floor. First, tense the muscles in your face, and hold this tension for a few seconds. Then relax completely. Now gradually move to your neck and tense the muscles. Then relax completely.

2. Repeat this exercise in different sections of the

body by working down through the shoulders, arms, chest, stomach, buttocks, thighs, and calves. By the time you reach your feet, you will almost surely be in a relaxed state.

3. As a variation, tense all the muscles of your body and then relax them all at the same time. You could also tense a particular muscle and then relax and gently massage it.

4. When you release tension, let your breath out, accompanied by a long "aaahh" or a sigh. This will help you get in touch with your deeper feelings and help you release them.

5. Quiet, deep breathing can follow this exercise.

III. Progressive Relaxation Exercise (2)

1. Sit in a comfortable position, either in a straight-backed chair or on a meditation cushion. Close your eyes and focus on your breath. Take full and easy breaths. As you inhale, feel life-giving oxygen flow into your lungs. As you exhale, feel your body relax. With each exhalation, you will feel your body relax more and more.

2. Feel your shoulders, your buttocks, your legs and feet, your belly, your arms and hands, your head, face, and jaw-relax. Tension is progressively leaving your body, and will continue to do so throughout this exercise.

3. Feel your mind release as well. Imagine that your mind is becoming freer, more open, and more alert.

4. Slowly let go of any anxieties, emotional tension, and fears with each exhalation of your breath. Feel yourself becoming emotionally relaxed as you exhale. Say to yourself, "I am relaxing." Continue this process for five minutes, or until you reach a level of deep relaxation.

4. Breathing

Although we all breathe, we usually view the rhythm of our breathing as automatic. We are seldom aware of the quality of our breathing. Without being conscious of it, we often hold our breath or take light, shallow, or quick breaths, especially when tense, fearful, or nervous.

Try the following: Consciously, take a few short, shallow, and irregular breaths. Be aware of how you feel. Chances are you will feel anxious, uneasy, and ungrounded. Now take a few deep, full breaths, counting to six at each inhalation and to six at each exhalation. The deeper, slower breathing will most likely help you feel more calm and comfortable.

When rapid, shallow breathing becomes habitual or chronic, we limit the amount of air that we take into our body. This not only impairs our body's ability to oxygenate the blood and other vital tissues, but can make us feel nervous, mentally sluggish, and tired. Deep, rhythmic breathing is essential for proper oxygenation, and can have a positive impact on how we feel mentally and emotionally. A number of simple breathing techniques follow.

The Awareness Breath Sit comfortably. Gently inhale while you do a slow count to four (approximately four seconds). Hold your breath quietly for a count of two, and then slowly exhale for a count of four.

As you breathe, your mind will probably begin to wander. Simply be aware of this and gently bring yourself back to your breath. By constantly directing your thought back to your breath, you are building a "muscle" of attentiveness and focus that will help you in your daily activities.

The Counting Breath With practice, the following breathing methods will enable you to relax whenever you feel nervous or anxious. You can perform one or more at any place or time. They can also lay the foundation for meditation practice.

1. Sit in a comfortable position. Gently inhale while you do a slow count to four (approximately four seconds); hold your breath quietly for a count of two, and then slowly exhale for a count of four. You can easily extend this breathing for a longer period, counting to six or even eight, while holding your breath for a count of four. Remember that such breaths should never be forced or uncomfortable. Breathe with awareness, and feel the life-giving oxygen being drawn into your body. As you exhale, imagine your body being cleansed.

2. Sitting comfortably as you inhale, count "One, one, one, one . . ." and count "Two, two, two, two . . ." as you exhale slowly. Then count "Three, three, three, three . . ." as you slowly fill your lungs again with air. Continue this process up to the count of ten, and then begin again from "one."

3. As you inhale, slowly count to ten, and then count to ten again as you exhale. Repeat this process as many times as you need, in order to fully concentrate on your breathing.

4. Another method involves counting "one" while you both inhale and exhale, so that each complete breath counts as one number. After one complete inhalation and exhalation, begin again and count "two" for your second full breath. Continue to count your breaths up to the number "ten" and then begin again from "one."

The Standing Breath Stand comfortably with your spine straight, your knees slightly bent, inhaling slowly and deeply through your nose. Make sure that you are breathing into your abdomen rather than your chest; place your hand on your belly to feel the air expand it as you inhale; gently pull in your stomach muscles as you exhale.

As you inhale, see in your mind's eye that you are sur-rounded by a brilliant golden light that is flowing into your body toward your abdomen and onward through the rest of your body, including your hands and feet. After inhaling, hold your breath and slowly count to three-with each count standing for one second. (With practice, you should be able to hold your breath for up to ten seconds.) Slowly exhale through your mouth, feeling any tensions in your body melt away. Yawn and stretch. Repeat this exercise three times.

The Yogi Complete Breath Learning how to breathe in a way that involves both the upper and lower parts of the lungs has been viewed as vital by yogis for centuries. Perhaps the most important breath to learn is known as "The Yogi Complete Breath," first introduced to the West by Yogi Ramacharaka in the early part of the twentieth century. He described performing this breath as follows:

> *Stand or sit erect. Breathing through the nostrils, inhale steadily, first filling the lower part of the lungs, which is accompanied by bringing into play the diaphragm, while [distending] exerts a gentle pressure on the abdominal organs, pushing forward the front walls of the abdomen. Then fill the middle part of the lungs, pushing out the lower ribs, breastbone, and chest. Then fill the higher portion of the lungs, protruding the upper chest, thus lifting the chest, including the upper six or seven pairs of ribs. In the final movement, the lower part of the abdomen will be slightly drawn in, which movement gives the lungs support and also helps to fill the highest part of the lungs.*

In The Science of Breath, Yogi Ramacharaka reminds us that this breath does not consist of three distinct movements, but is rather one continuous, fluid movement. He recommends that we retain the breath for a couple of seconds and then exhale slowly, drawing in the abdomen slightly as the air leaves the lungs, and relaxing the chest and abdomen after releasing the air.

You can do The Yogi Complete Breath whenever you feel like it, though at first you may want to do it during a period of quiet contemplation, or just before beginning your daily meditation. Gradually, you can begin consciously breathing fully and deeply in more and more of your daily activities, until deep, rhythmic breathing becomes a normal part of your life.

Only living people breathe. Dead people don't. The more we breathe, the more alive we are. And the more we practice deep, rhythmic breathing, the more we partake of oxygen: the essence of life itself.

5. Keeping a Journal

While not considered an essential part of meditation, writing your experiences in a journal can be helpful for anyone interested in meditation. On one hand, the journal can help remind you of your actual experience with different meditation methods, thus allowing you to improve your techniques. It also helps you to enjoy deeper insights into yourself: what makes you impatient, how you breathe, what areas in your body cause you difficulty. Finally, the journal is an excellent place for you to record valuable impressions, ideas, and insights that may have come to you during your meditation practice. When left to memory alone, much valuable information can be lost. Your journal allows you to maintain a permanent record of your insights and experiences, to which you can easily refer.

The way you maintain a journal is entirely up to you. Some people record the date, time, and subject of the meditation, with additional sections devoted to realizations and difficulties that come up during it. A sample journal entry:

> *Date: January 25*
> *Time: 8–8:20 a.m.*
> *Subject: Candle meditation*
> *Difficulties: I lost track of my breathing during the relaxation exercise, and had to return to it several times. It was difficult to relax at first. While looking at the candle, I spaced out a few times.*
>
> *Realizations: I never realized how beautiful a candle can be. I felt inspired and calmed by the flame. I want to burn candles at the table when I have dinner with my husband. So romantic!*

Chapter Two: Meditations from Various Disciplines

Meditations on Sacred Symbols

Sacred symbols express a meaning without words. Many, such as the cross or swastika, are specific to certain ancient religions and cultures, while others, like a lighted candle, have universal meanings. Many symbols will have specific meanings to the individual: A devout Christian will have a very different impression of a cross than would a practicing Jew. However, when you do this meditation, try to move past any preconceived ideas you may have about a particular symbol.

1. After doing one of the Basic Relaxation Exercises described earlier, choose a sacred symbol on which to meditate. You can either use a picture of a symbol, or visualize the symbol in your mind's eye. Before choosing a sacred symbol, you may want to spend some time studying its sacred meanings. The following are some possible symbols on which to meditate (along with their meanings):

 Ankh ✳ immortality; the primordial movement and state of cosmic being

 Cross ✳ eternal life; union of spirit and matter

 Diamond ✳ the many facets of Divine wisdom

حقا يق بسيا رى زهمت الهى الماس

 Five-pointed star ✳ a symbol of humanity

 Lotus ✳ a universal symbol; creation and spiritual realization

 Star of David ✳ the unity of the masculine and feminine aspects of nature

Triangle ✱ the trinity—father, son, and holy spirit;
upper point—one life, two sides—duality of existence,
base—offspring of spirit and matter

 Yin and yang ✱ dynamic balance between the
masculine and the feminine

Some other symbols:

Crescent ✱ the Moon; emblem of Isis, the Egyptian
Earth goddess
Disc ✱ the cosmic egg; the entire cosmic process
by which worlds and living beings are born
Line/Horizontal ✱ matter, Earth
Line/Vertical ✱ spirit, Godhead
Snake ✱ wisdom
Spiral ✱ action in ascending spirit
Symbol of Change ✱ from the I-Ching
Tree ✱ grounded in the Earth, with branches reaching
toward heaven

2. Devote between five and ten minutes to the sacred
symbol, allowing your mind to ponder its structure, form,
and meaning; chances are that new and unexpected ideas

and impressions will come into your mind. If you wish, you can later record your impressions in your journal.

3. As you conclude your meditation, take several deep breaths and stretch your body. Slowly rise from your meditation posture.

Energy Meditations

The following meditations are designed to enable you to safely access the energy of the universe, known in the East as chi or prana. Although best done in the morning, they can be performed whenever you feel the need for more energy during the course of the day.

Contacting Universal Energy

1. Seated comfortably in a straight-backed chair or on a cushion or mat, and do one of the Basic Relaxation Exercises. Continue to pay attention to your breathing; close your eyes.

2. Visualize yourself flying upward like a soaring bird. Light is shining all around you. Feel the radiance and warmth of this dazzling, bright light. Feel this light flowing through you, bathing you with energy. This energy brings with it a sense of inner peace and well-being. Acknowledge that this light not only invigorates you, but guides you in making the correct choices in your life as well. Continue to be aware of your breathing.

4. After several minutes, visualize yourself descending to Earth again, yet continue to feel some of this bright light within you. Open your eyes and slowly come out of your meditation.

With a brief expression of thanks to the Great Spirit, you are now ready to begin your day!

Illumination Meditation

1. Sit comfortably in a straight-backed chair or on a cushion or mat. Perform one of the Basic Relaxation Exercises, being especially aware of your breathing.

2. Visualize your body and mind as being a dark-gray mass, totally devoid of light. Feel the heaviness, the emptiness, the lack of energy and inspiration. Allow this feeling to continue for a minute or two.

3. Now, imagine a tiny source of pure, white light beginning to shine within you. It can originate in your heart, at the base of your spine, in your brain, or in any other part of your body.

4. Imagine this light growing in size and brightness. Feel its warmth and healing. See this light expand while it permeates your entire body with light, including your arms, legs, fingers and toes. As you breathe, see this light radiating outward, filling the atmosphere with its energy and warmth.

5. Now, mentally reduce the force until you feel the core of light and its radiance filling your entire body.

6. Quietly conclude your meditation while retaining the feeling of being filled with light. Take a few deep breaths and stretch before getting up from your seated position.

Mantra Meditation

We live in a world of sound. Sound is essentially a form of energy that is transmitted through air and other conductors. Soothing sounds can range from the movement of the wind through the trees to the gurgling of a stream to the breaking of waves on a rocky shore. Other pleasant sounds include the quiet ringing of bells. Discordant sounds, like the screeching of brakes or the incessant barking of a dog, tend to inhibit our ability to think clearly. Noise pollution affects us physically, emotionally, and mentally, often producing stress and feelings of ungroundedness.

By the same token, human speech can also have a powerful impact in our daily lives; we really know very little about how it affects us. Speech tones, volume, and certain words are types of energy that make us react in different ways. In some cases, a hateful word or a careless phrase can hurt us even more than getting punched in the stomach.

The human voice has long played a role in religious practices throughout the world. Chanting, praying, and singing are all powerful methods of using voice vibration and the power of sound to elevate our consciousness and make us more receptive to spiritual forces. Singing spiritual hymns and chanting heartfelt prayers and the holy names of God have always been viewed as an essential part of daily spiritual practice. Serious devotees of the spiritual life, from Catholic monks to Hindu yogis, Jewish kabbalists to Tibetan Buddhist monks, have a powerful tradition of chanting that has survived to this day.

The word mantra comes from the Sanskrit, meaning "the thought that liberates and protects." Using a mantra in spiritual practice involves chanting, singing, or even humming a sacred sound that can either help prepare the foundation for meditation, or elevate our consciousness during meditation itself. A mantra involves the repetition of the name of God, such as Ave Maria by the Christians or Elohim by the Jews. Chanting the name of Jesus has been a vital aspect of Christian meditation, while chanting the name of the goddess Oshoun or the god Oshala has been practiced by adherents to African religions like Macumba, and the Brazilian Candomble. It can also involve repeating a sacred word like shanti or peace.

Aside from the vibration of the actual names or sacred words, a mantra can have powerful personal associations. For Muslims, there is no word more meaningful than Allah, while the word Aum or Om is viewed by Hindus as symbolizing the essence of spiritual reality. Yet we must beware of mechanically reciting a mantra or any sacred sound. The power of a mantra is proportionate to the feeling that we put into its expression. For this reason, our personal choice of a mantra is extremely important; it should ideally be a sacred word or name that we can personally relate to.

Having said this, many mantras are universal in scope. Based on the idea that there is no such thing as a "Jewish soul" or a "Christian soul," but rather a "Divine Soul," the actual mantra is unimportant; any sacred word or name can impart a powerful spiritual vibration and uplift the consciousness of any receptive individual.

Reciting a mantra produces the following benefits:
* It calms the mind and the emotions.
* It elevates the consciousness.
* The breath becomes more regular and controlled.
* Mantras are vehicles for expressing our deepest emotions and yearnings.
* Mantras "feed" the higher self and allow it to play a larger role in our daily life.

Advice on Chanting

When you recite a mantra, gently pull in your abdominal muscles, allowing your chest to widen as you vocalize. Breathe through your nose. Exhale evenly while paying attention to your breath. The "melody" of the mantra needs to be consistent and should not change with each vocalization.

Vocalizing a sacred word in a low, gentle tone increases its power. However, if you find yourself in a place where chanting a mantra is not appropriate (such as a bus or another public place), you can recite the sound mentally, and envision it totally enveloping your being as if you were making the sound with your voice.

Christian Mantra

The Ave Maria is an expression of love and devotion toward the Virgin Mary, the mother of Jesus. It is a powerful mantra that can be vocalized either aloud or silently.

Hail Mary, full of Grace,
The Lord is with thee.
Blessed art thou amongst women
And Blessed is the fruit of thy womb, Jesus.
Holy Mary, Mother of God,
Pray for us sinners,
Now, and in the hour of our death

Another Christian prayer that was designed to pray without ceasing, making it well-suited to be used as a mantra is the Jesus Prayer:

Lord Jesus Christ, Son of God,
Have mercy on me, a sinner.

Arabic Mantra

la illaha illa? llah (There is no God but Allah.)

Allah Akbar (There is no one greater than Allah.)

Allah

Hebrew Mantras

Elohim (Great Living One)

Kodosh (Holy One)

Adonai (Lord)

Ahavah (Love)

Shalom (Peace)

Ribbono shel Olem (Master of the Universe or Source and Substance of All Reality)

Hindu and Buddhist Mantras

Om is a most sacred mantra, and means "the divine energy." It represents the trinity of the physical, mental, and spiritual aspects of our being, as well as an individual, universal, and transcendental consciousness.

The "o" and the "m" should be sounded for fifteen seconds each, making a total of thirty seconds (be sure to inhale deeply before beginning the mantra). H. Saraydarian suggests that we vocalize Om three times before beginning meditation and three times after we complete meditation. He recommends that the first Om be vocalized softly, the second Om louder, and the third still louder. After the three Oms are sounded solemnly, we should visualize their effects during a period of silence. Om can also be sounded silently. If you have heard others recite this mantra (especially a guru or yoga teacher), recall how it sounds and reproduce the sound in your mind. A graphic of this sacred word is written in Sanskrit below.

Hari Om is considered the mantra for healing; one that will preserve the body and mind in a state of health so that we can attain spiritual realization. In Hindu mythology, Hari is the name for the god Vishnu, "the preserver" of the spirit. Chanting "Hari" is also viewed as a sign of repentance for our disharmonious actions and attitudes. This mantra can be chanted once per breath, or two sequences per breath to strengthen concentration.

Om Shanti combines the sacred Om with the Sanskrit word for "peace," not unlike the Hebrew word shalom. The words can also be reversed, recited as "Shanti Om."

Om Mani Padmi Hum means "The Jewel of the Lotus," and symbolizes completion and integration. A very powerful mantra, it should be recited slowly, but in one complete breath.

Om Nama Sivaya is believed to help destroy ignorance. It asks God to help us transform our negative qualities and destroy the obstacles to living a spiritual life. Like the previous mantra, it should be vocalized slowly in one breath.

Om Krishna Guru is recommended when you are seeing a spiritual teacher, either on the concrete level, or as a spirit guide. In addition to "Om" meaning the Supreme Energy,

"Krishna" is said to represent the supreme energy manifested in a form that becomes personal to us. "Guru" is the Sanskrit term for spiritual teacher.

Om Ah Hung is a mantra used primarily by Tibetan Buddhists. In Buddhism, "Ah" is the source of all speech and sound; it is also a sound of purification, warmth, and healing. It represents the energy of expansion and empowerment. "Hung" (pronounced hoong with a soft h) is a sound of infinity, enlightenment, and Oneness. When Om, Ah, and Hung are recited together, the Tibetan monk Tulku Thondup suggests that the length of each sacred word may be varied.

Om Sri Rama Jaya Rama is an appeal to the soul to live according to Divine Will. In the Hindu religion, the god Rama represents the king or pillar. As a "call to victory" of the higher self, this mantra is ideal for a person seeking transformation and self-realization. Another related mantra would be Hare Rama.

Aum is closely related to Om. Swami Sivananda taught that the cosmic Aum is traditionally chanted in three parts, with equal time devoted to each part. When you chant this sacred sound, visualize the Ah being chanted in the area of your body near the navel; the oo, just above the diaphragm, and the mm at the base of the throat. Like the Om, this mantra should be done slowly and clearly in one long complete breath.

Aum Nama Bhagavate Gajananaya Namah is a mantra used to invoke the presence of the god Ganesha, whose power is believed to remove obstacles and to provide clarity and wisdom when we need to make an important decision.

Radha Govinda is a mantra used to discover the Divine within. It is to be chanted with intense feelings of love and devotion, as if the mantra is the key that will open a buried treasure. In Hindu mythology, Radha was the lover of Lord Krishna and is seen as a symbol of unceasing love for God.

Judeo Christian Mantras

Shalom is one of the most important and beautiful words in the Hebrew language. When used as a mantra, you can elongate the syllables so it is expressed as:

shhhhaaa

looooo

mmmmm

not unlike the Om described earlier. The syllables can be pronounced in equal lengths, or in varying lengths. The mantra can be chanted in one long breath if desired.

Your Basic Mantra Meditation Technique

As with any other form of mediation, take a few moments to

relax, using one of the Basic Relaxation Exercises described earlier. While sitting or standing in a comfortable position, choose a mantra that has significance to you. Recite it aloud clearly and with awareness of your outgoing breath. Remember that different mantras may require a specific form of expression, so refer to the guidelines for the specific mantras offered above. Allow the sound to permeate the surrounding atmosphere and vibrate deep within your body and mind, so that you feel the power of the manta completely envelop your being.

At first, recite the mantra for several minutes; with practice, you may want to extend your chanting to a half hour or more.

When you wish to stop chanting, make your final recitation and devote several minutes to quiet, rhythmic breathing. You may wish to say a short prayer before you conclude the meditation.

Intoning the Name of a Buddha: Namo Amitabha

The repeated intoning of the name of a Buddha is a powerful method of focusing the mind and calming the emotions. The phrase Namo Amitabha, means "taking refuge in boundless life and enlightenment." The following mantra meditation was inspired by the technique taught by the Won school of Buddhism in Korea. It is intended to help us discover the Amitabha of our own minds and return to the paradise of our own original nature.

1. Sit on a straight-backed chair or on a comfortable cushion placed on the floor. Maintain an upright posture and relax your body and mind. Do not swing or shake your body. You may wish to do one of the Basic Relaxation Exercises described earlier before you begin chanting. You may also want to use sacred beads for counting each chant as you recite it.

2. Speaking in your normal voice, concentrate your mind, body, and spirit on intoning the name of a Buddha, linking your entire being with the phrase Namo Amitabha. Recite the phrase slowly and clearly with each outward breath. Merely verbally intoning Namo Amitabha without concentration of thought is said to be of little effect, but the silent repetition of the name of a Buddha can be very powerful if you do it consciously.

3. Allow your mind to relax completely as you chant. Do not imagine the figure of Buddha as something you seek from outside, but allow the words to surround you totally, bringing life to your own innate Buddha nature.

4. Continue this chanting meditation for five minutes at first. With practice, you can extend your meditation to ten minutes or longer.

5. When you are finished, take several deep breaths and slowly rise from your seated position.

Teachers of Won Buddhism suggest that you intone the

name of the Buddha whenever you are annoyed by "delusive thoughts," involving emotions like greed, envy, or fear, or while you are walking, standing, sitting, or reclining; however you should not chant the Buddha's name if it will distract you from what you are doing, such as driving a car or operating machinery.

CD Assist

An enjoyable and inspiring method of practicing mantra meditation is with the aid of a CD. Many spiritual organizations as well as noted spiritual teachers produce such CDs.

After doing one of the Basic Relaxation Exercises, sit comfortably and turn on the CD, using either earphones or speakers. Recite the mantra along with the voice(s) on the CD, remaining aware of your breathing and any areas of tension in your body or mind. As you recite the mantra, feel these tensions dissolve.

Allow yourself to fully participate in your experience, yet maintain awareness and a sense of being grounded. You may want to move your body to the words and music in a form of sacred dance. If you wish to dance, make sure there is plenty of room, so that you don't knock into anything. Some people can completely lose themselves in a trance-dance, in the rhythm and repetition; their bodies keeps moving, but they fall into a meditative state. It is important to strive to retain awareness during this and all other types of meditative practice.

Mantra as Prayer

Some mantras may be in the form of many words organized to produce a special effect, not unlike a prayer. One such mantra is recited during group meditation by members of the Meditation Group for the New Age in Ojai, California:

> One Source, One Power
> Thou in Whom we live and move
>   and have our being,
> The Power Whom can make
>   all things new,
> Give of thine abundance:
>   of vision and insight
>   of wisdom and joy
>   of health and vitality
>   of efficient coworkers
>   of all the resources necessary
> In order that the Work may be adequate
>   to the growing needs
> And the great opportunities
>   of the present time
> With faith, we give thanks.

The Great Invocation is another powerful mantra that can be an important aspect of any meditation or prayer service. Invoking the forces of Light, Love, and Power, the mantra not only strengthens these qualities in the world, but within our own being as well.

Before actually reciting this mantra, take some time to study the meaning of each line. As we develop a greater understanding and appreciation of its power, it will have more power when we recite it.

Recite each line of this mantra carefully and in one breath. As you speak, strive to visualize the image that each line creates in your heart and mind.

> From the point of Light within the Mind of God
> Let light stream forth into the minds of men.
> Let Light descend on Earth.
> From the point of Love within the Heart of God
> Let love stream forth into the hearts of men.
> May Christ return to Earth.
> From the center where the Will of God is known
> Let purpose guide the little wills of men;
> The purpose which the Masters know and serve.
> From the center which we call the race of men
> Let the Plan of Love and Light work out
> And may it seal the door where evil dwells.
> Let Light and Love and Power restore the Plan on Earth.

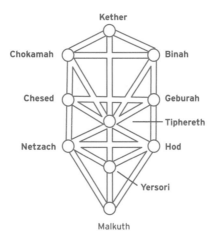

Kether

Chokamah   Binah

Chesed   Geburah

Tiphereth

Netzach   Hod

Yersori

Malkuth

Tree of Life-Kabbalah Meditation

In the Kabbalah, the ancient system of Jewish mysticism, the date palm represented the symbolic Tree of Life, known as Sephiroth. It is made up of the ten emanations of the infinite God, or the "qualities of God's infinity made manifest in a finite world."

To symbolize the manifestation of the cosmos from a single transcendent source, the Sephirothic Tree is inverted. Each of the ten Sephira represents a group of exalted ideas, titles, and attributes, as follows:

Kether ✳ 1st Sephira, the crown or the primordial point

Chokmah ✳ 2nd Sephira, wisdom or the primordial idea

Binah ✳ 3rd Sephira, intelligence and understanding

Chesed or Gedula ✳ 4th Sephira, mercy or love

Geburah ✳ 5th Sephira, the "power" of God, manifested
　　　　as severity, strength, fortitude, and justice

Tipereth ✳ 6th Sephira, compassion, beauty, the heart
　　　　and center of the Sephirothic Tree

Netzach ✳ 7th Sephira, firmness, victory, or lasting
　　　　endurance

Hod ✳ 8th Sephira, glory or majesty

Yesod ✳ 9th Sephira, formation, or the foundation/basis
　　　　of all active forces in God

Malkuth ✳ 10th Sephira, the kingdom of Earth, action,
　　　　and all nature

Kabbalists consider the Sephiroth to be a bridge connect-
ing the finite universe with the infinite God. In the Zohar, a
compendium of kabbalistic teachings, it is said that the Torah
is the Sephirothic Tree of Life and that all who occupy themselves with it are assured of life in the world to come.

The Meditation

Before beginning this meditation, you may wish to light a
white votive candle.

1. Do one of the Basic Relaxation Exercises.

2. Have before you an image of the Sephiroth. Choose one of the Divine Attributes, close your eyes, and ponder it for several minutes. You may choose an attribute each day according to your intuition, or meditate on a different attribute daily in numerical order.

3. During your meditation, allow your mind to make whatever associations or connections it will.

4. At the conclusion of your meditation, record your observations in a journal.

Chapter Three:
Buddhist Meditations

Basic Zazen Meditation

An aspect of Zen Buddhism, Zazen, or "sitting meditation," places emphasis on direct seeing through sitting quietly and not thinking. The following meditation method is based on the teachings of the Japanese Zen master Dogen Zenji.

Place

Zazen, as with other meditations, should be practiced in a quiet place where you can meditate without disturbances.

The room should be moderately lit, warm in winter and cool in summer, and kept clean. Ideally, this space should contain a picture or statue of the Buddha. Fresh flowers and incense should be placed in front of the image.

Preparing for Meditation: Five Suggestions

When doing Zazen, meditation instructors recommend the following guidelines:

1. Do not meditate if you haven't had sufficient sleep or if you are very tired.

2. Avoid overeating and excessive alcohol consumption before sitting.

3. Wash your hands and face before sitting.

4. Wear clean, loose-fitting garments.

5. Place a thick mat (known in Japan as a zaniku) in front of the wall and place a cushion (zafu) on top of it. Sit cross-legged on the zafu, placing the base of your spine at the center so that half of the zafu is behind you. Rest your knees firmly on the zaniku.

Body Position

If possible, sit in the full lotus position described earlier, known in Japan as kekkafuza. If this is too difficult, sit in the half-lotus position, known as hankafuza. In either of these positions, you can rest both knees on the zaniku.

Posture

Straighten the lower part of your back, push your buttocks outward, and push your hips forward. Straighten your spine, but not so much that you feel uncomfortable.

Pull in your chin and extend your neck as though reaching to the ceiling. Your ears should be parallel to your shoulders. Your nose should be in-line with your navel. After straightening your back, relax your shoulders, back, and abdomen without changing your posture. Sit up straight, leaning neither to the right nor left, neither forward nor backward.

Position of Hands

Moving your hands near your lap, place your right hand (palm up) on your left foot, and your left hand on your right palm. The tips of your thumbs should touch each other lightly. This position is called Cosmic Mudra or hokkaijoin. Place the tips of your thumbs in front of your navel, holding your arms slightly apart from your body.

The Mouth

In Zazen, the mouth is kept closed. Place your tongue lightly against the roof of your mouth.

The Eyes

Zen masters recommend that you keep your eyes slightly open, with your vision cast down at about a 45-degree angle in front of you. Without focusing on anything in particular, allow your field of vision to encompass everything in front of you. If your eyes are closed, it is easier to daydream or become drowsy.

Breathing

Begin your breathing by quietly making a deep exhalation and inhalation. Then open your mouth slightly and exhale slowly and smoothly. In order to expel all the air from your lungs, exhale from your abdomen, pulling the abdomen in slowly. Then close your mouth and inhale through your nose naturally. This form of breathing is known in Japanese as kanki-issoku.

Continue doing abdominal breathing through your nose during meditation. Do not try to control your breathing, but allow it to happen naturally. Allow your long breaths to be even and long, and short breaths to be short; strive to become aware of the difference. Your breathing should be so quiet that others cannot hear you. Beginners may wish to count their breaths, which will increase awareness and help regulate breathing.

Swaying the Body

When you feel the need, swaying the body can be a part of Zazen meditation. Place your hands palms up on your knees and gently sway the upper part of your body from side to side. You can do this several times. Without moving your hips, move your trunk as though it were a long, flexible pole leaning to the right and to the left, so that you stretch your hip muscles. You may also sway forward and backward.

As you sway, let each movement become smaller and smaller until it ceases with your body in an upright position. This exercise should take several minutes. At this point, assume the Cosmic Mudra position with your hands once more.

Awareness

During meditation, do not concentrate on any particular subject or attempt to control your thinking. By maintaining the proper posture, and as your breathing settles down, your mind will become quiet as well.

If thoughts come up, don't struggle with them or try to escape from them. Simply leave them alone, and allow them to come and go freely. The goal here is to awaken from distraction or drowsiness and return to the correct posture and breathing, moment by moment.

Completing Zazen

When you finish Zazen, bow, place your hands palms up on your thighs, and gently sway your body (left to right, right to left, and forward and backward) a few times. Then sway a bit more extensively, so that you actually feel your muscles stretching. Take a deep breath. Slowly unfold your legs. Stand up slowly and carefully, especially if your legs are asleep.

The Eight-Fold Path Meditation

According to traditional Buddhist teachings, the way of liber-
ation is "The Noble Eight-Fold Path." Less a religious doc-
trine than a form of moral psychology, the eight factors are:

1. Right understanding, or knowledge of the true
nature of existence.

2. Right thought, or thought that is free from negativity, ill will, and cruelty. Right thought also involves
being aware of our inaccurate, separative, or destructive
beliefs.

3. Right speech, calling for speech that is not only
true, kind, and helpful, but speech that does not contain
gossip, harshness, or idle chitchat.

4. Right action, involving not just the avoidance of
killing, stealing, and adultery, but being involved in personal, political, and social activities that heal, nourish,
and alleviate pain in the world.

5. Right livelihood, involving an occupation that
does no harm to conscious living beings, but also a voca-
tion or avocation that does good for society and benefits
the Earth.

6. Right effort, which involves not only cultivating
wholesome qualities in ourselves, but getting involved in
activities that benefit other living beings.

7. Right mindfulness, which involves developing

mental awareness and clarity; it also calls upon us to focus on ideas and concepts that are important in life, as opposed to devoting our thoughts to worry, trivia, or celebrity gossip.

8. Right concentration, calling for the cultivation of a mind that is both collected and focused through meditation.

The following meditation plan is designed to be used over a period of eight days. Each day is devoted to meditating on one aspect of The Noble Eight-Fold Path. For this meditation, you will need a notebook and a picture or other image of the Buddha. You may also wish to write down each aspect of The Eight-Fold Path on an index card to refer to during meditation.

1. Seat yourself comfortably in a chair or on a cushion on the floor. Perform one of the Basic Relaxation Exercises described earlier. Be aware of your breathing, which should be deep, slow, and even.

2. With the Buddha image before you, pray for clarity and enlightenment. This can be a short prayer like, "I pray to open myself to the wisdom of The Noble Eight-Fold Path and learn to follow it in my daily life."

3. Choose an aspect of The Noble Eight-Fold Path and read the card on which you wrote the word. Ponder the meaning and ramifications of this aspect carefully. Ask about its meaning. To what extent do you manifest it in your life? In what areas is your understanding and practice lacking? Be totally honest with yourself, allowing your thoughts to flow freely, writing them down in your notebook. At the same time, strive to be objective, being aware of feelings of pride, remorse, or guilt that may come up. Devote five to ten minutes to this exercise.

4. When you are ready to conclude your meditation, take a few deep breaths. Express gratitude for your insights. Gently stretch your body as you slowly rise from your meditation posture.

T'ai Chi Chuan Meditation

T'ai Chi Chuan is a Chinese system of exercise and movement meditation developed hundreds of years ago by Taoist monks. The practice of T'ai Chi involves special breathing techniques and a set of eighty-one movements, which involve nearly every part of the body, including hands and fingers, feet and toes, and even eyes and buttocks. The movements are done very slowly with each flowing into the next—one long, continuous movement. Although to observers it appears to be a very relaxed form of meditative movement, T'ai Chi involves tremendous inner focus and concentration. A major goal of this practice is to gather life energy, known as chi, into the lower abdomen, and distribute it freely to the arms, legs, and the rest of the body. This enables the body to achieve a balance of yin and yang energy, which is believed to enhance overall health and provide mental, emotional, and spiritual harmony.

Medical research carried out both in China and the West has found that the regular practice of T'ai Chi Chuan can lower stress and blood pressure; enhance respiratory capacity and increase oxygen delivery to body cells; improve immune function, digestion, leg strength, and balance; and reduce falls among the elderly.

Millions of Chinese practice T'ai Chi on a daily basis, and an increasing number of Westerners also utilize it as an important meditative practice, especially those who dislike remaining in a sitting position. In addition to its tranquilizing effect on our emotions, it enables us to get more in touch with the life energy in the universe and in our own bodies. T'ai Chi also helps us conserve energy and produce a feeling of physical confidence and emotional security.

Like many forms of the martial arts, T'ai Chi cannot be taught from a book such as this one. However, a variety of DVDs are available in stores and public libraries, and T'ai Chi classes are easy to find in many cities and towns. You can find instruction in such places as martial arts academies, health clubs, YMCAs, meditation schools, senior centers, and adult education classes. High schools and universities also often provide classes in T'ai Chi.

Chakra Meditations

In the Hindu and Buddhist traditions, our bodies contain seven energy centers. Each energy center is called a chakra—from the Sanskrit word for "wheel." Each chakra is a swirling center of energy, and has a specific role to play in our lives. We possess seven major chakras, which correspond with seven glands or organs, as seen below.

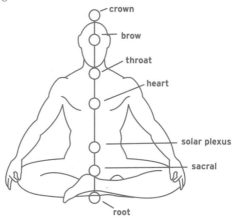

We need to understand the functions of chakras because they often respond to our attitudes and feelings, and in turn affect us in both subtle and not-so-subtle ways. When open, a chakra receives or transmits energy that corresponds to the qualities represented by the specific chakra. When a chakra is blocked or closed, we are cut off from that particular energy.

Becoming more aware of where the chakras are and how they function, we can better understand the hidden factors that affect how we think and feel, how we relate to others, and why others relate to us as they do. We can then consciously work to gradually open these energy centers, and gain greater balance and harmony in our lives and relationships.

The Root Chakra 5/12/2010

The root chakra is located at the base of the spine. It is the energy center that is related to the amount of physical energy we have as well as our will to live. When the life force is fully functioning through this center, we have a strong ability to deal with physical reality. We are "grounded" in the world. However, when this chakra is blocked, we experience a low level of physical vitality and will probably not make a strong impression in the world.

The Sacral Chakra

The sacral chakra is located in the area of the body near the navel. It is connected with the sexual glands, and regulates both the amount and the quality of our sexual energy. When this chakra is open, it provides us with a strong sex drive and a correspondingly strong desire for sexual union. Just before we consciously find ourselves sexually excited, we often experience a "tingling" feeling in the sacral area. This is the preparation of the sacral chakra.

When this chakra is blocked due to emotional problems or negative attitudes, the entire sex life is depressed, and the sexual act has little physical appeal. Women who have a severe block in this chakra are unable to achieve orgasm, and often find penetration painful. Men with a blocked chakra are prone to chronic impotence, premature ejaculation, or general disinterest in sex.

The Solar Plexus Chakra

The third energy center, the solar plexus chakra, is located in the diaphragm region towards the center of the body. This chakra governs our feeling nature, and is closely linked to our emotions. If we have an open solar plexus center, we have a rich emotional life. When it is blocked, we often cannot feel emotionally. In many cases, a block in this chakra can cut off the energy flowing from the sacral chakra to the heart chakra, which makes us feel "cut off" from our partner during sex. When this occurs, sex will not be connected to love, and love feelings will not contain a sexual component.

This chakra is also connected to instinctual perception. When we speak of having "gut feelings," we are describing one of the functions of the solar plexus chakra.

The Heart Chakra

The fourth, or heart, chakra is located in the center of the chest near the thymus gland. It is the energy center through which we love and see the inner beauty of others. To the degree that this center is open and functioning, we have the ability to love others. Being the home of romantic love, self-lessness, and compassion, it is the most important energy center for us to develop at our present stage of evolution.

When we experience deep love, we may feel a "flutter" in the heart region. This is the heart chakra. When we lose a loved one, we can feel pain in the heart area. The heart chakra may actually be wounded, and its functioning can be impaired—the term "to die of a broken heart" is believed by some to be more than a literary reference.

When the heart chakra is closed or blocked, the individual has problems loving others. They are often cold or calculating, and rarely give without expecting something in return.

The Throat Chakra

The fifth, or throat, chakra's location corresponds to that of the thyroid gland. It is seen primarily as a receptive energy center, related to the power of clear audience or psychic hearing. Through this chakra we receive impressions from the world around us: if our view of the world is positive, we will receive nourishment through this energy center. However, if our perceptions are negative, we will attract negativity. When this chakra is closed or blocked, we have difficulty "taking things in," whether they are new observations, unfamiliar ideas, or the feelings of others.

The throat is also the active creative center. The words we speak—even in ordinary conversation—create our experiences, which can range from the most superficial (idle gossip) to the most profound. It is also the higher sexual chakra for the humanity of the future, when verbal exchange will be a major source of human creativity. In fact, the power of the word may even become as important as the physical exchange that now takes place between two people when they make love.

The Brow Chakra

The sixth chakra, or brow chakra, is located on the forehead between the eyes. Because it is often related to clairvoyance, it is also called "the third eye." This energy center is linked to the capacity to visualize and understand mental and spiritual concepts. When it is blocked or weak, the individual is often confused and can have false images about the reality of things. There may also be blocks in forming creative ideas. Clairvoyants and holistic healers believe that the abuse of drugs-especially over long periods of time-affects the functioning of this chakra in a very negative way.

The Crown Chakra

The seventh and most powerful energy center is known as the crown chakra, which is located at the top of the head. When we have developed this chakra, we have reached perfection in all our faculties, and have a direct link between the lower and higher planes of existence. The crown chakra symbolizes the connection to spirituality and the integration of our being on all levels, and as a result, it is fully energized only in spiritual masters and sages. This is where we remain connected to our soul. That is why the infant has a soft spot on the top of its head. Over the first year of life, as the child develops a sense of identity with the physical body, this spot gradually hardens.

Chakras and the Serpent Power

All of the energy centers we've just described are given the power of life by the creative force in the universe known as the Kundalini. Often called the "fire of passion," Kundalini is the fire energy in nature that gives rise to all creativity and passion. We take this life force into our bodies with every breath. We also take in this life force by eating fresh, raw foods.

Of all the elements, Fire symbolizes transformation: It takes something material and changes it into ashes and energy. The energy released by the fire doesn't cease to exist, but is transformed into a different manifestation. In our own bodies, we are constantly transforming this universal energy and using it in hundreds of different ways. We use the creative force not only to keep our bodies alive and moving, but also to eat, paint, walk down the street, work, heal, meditate, and make love. This is why metaphysics teaches that the Fire energy, or Kundalini, is a magical element with the unique power to transform.

Kundalini is also called the "Serpent Power," described in esoteric literature as a serpent lying dormant in each human being. It is often pictured as curled up at the base of the spine, the home of the root chakra. The serpent, because it has the ability to shed its skin, is a potent symbol of transformation. It is most often represented in Buddhist literature is the cobra. Through its lethal bite, it can take other life forms from the physical world and usher them through the portals of death to another dimension. Death is thus seen as a form of transformation.

Many ancient rituals (especially in the Tantric tradition) were devoted to awakening this serpent power so that it could gradually rise up through the spine. As it rises, this serpent power energizes the various chakras until it finally opens and awakens the spiritual centers in the head. When the Kundalini rises to higher chakras in our evolutionary process, we enter a new state of consciousness. We "die" to the old and embrace the next level of consciousness through this process of spiritual transformation.

Our energy centers are the voices of our development in the evolutionary process. In the early stages, we function only from the root chakra—the primitive person seeking only to survive. We sound only one note. As we evolve and grow, the higher chakras are energized one by one. As the Kundalini rises to higher chakras, we gradually become a melody of many notes, with their accompanying power and splendor.

When developed with care and awareness, the chakras provide energy, balance, and self-awareness. However, when they are stimulated artificially through drugs or through the unguided practice of certain types of Tantra yoga, they can be awakened prematurely by the Kundalini force. This often brings the person more energy than he or she can handle, and leads to imbalance on both physical and psychological levels. In extreme cases, it can result in insanity and even death.

For these reasons, it is very important to develop the chakras in order beginning with the root, because it is necessary to have a strong foundation to support awareness in the next chakra. You cannot put a roof on a house with no walls and a weak foundation, because the roof (and the entire house) will collapse. Similarly, the chakras must be continually balanced so that they are exchanging energy—thus keeping all channels of communication open to prevent imbalances. This allows us to use a strong chakra to support and heal a weaker one. Techniques like aura balancing and polarity therapy, which relax certain chakras while stimulating others, help us achieve a balance of energies throughout both our dense and subtle bodies.

As we meditate on the energy centers of the body, we arrive at a deeper understanding of how each of them functions in our own life. We can ask: Where am I blocked? Where am I overstimulated? What qualities do I need to develop that will bring greater balance and harmony within?

I Sending Light Form a triangle with your hands, using your thumbs and forefingers. Hold this triangle over the chakra you wish to stimulate. Visualize or feel a pulsating white light in the chakra inside this triangle. Repeat the sound "Hum" over and over, which will focus and stimulate the energy within.

The apex of the triangle should point downward when you're working with the root, sacral, and solar plexus chakras to ground and stabilize the energy of this white light. When working with the higher chakras, the apex of the triangle should point upward to inspire and uplift the light in the triangle.

When you do this exercise, begin at the root chakra and move upward to the crown chakra. After you have sent light into this energy center, move your way back down to the root chakra once more.

II Visualization This is a more advanced meditation that works best with those who already have had some practice with meditation and visualization.

As you sit in a meditative position, gently breathe in the Kundalini energy of the universe through your nose. Feel your breath go to the root chakra. Focus the breath there as you visualize a point of red energy. It is a single flame of hot, primal, dynamic power that will burst into activity in the higher chakras. Let your breath out again.

Now breathe in gently and focus on the sacral chakra.

Visualize two colored points (red on the right and blue on the left), which will then form a line of purple light. This symbolizes their procreative dominion over the Earth, and the union of the active and receptive, the yin and yang.

Next, focus your breath on the solar plexus. Visualize three points in the form of a triangle surrounding this chakra. The top point is yellow, and the base points are both red. See these colors merge to form the color orange. This figure symbolizes courage and illumination for action with understanding. It also empowers your feelings of joy and innocence.

Moving to the heart chakra, visualize a diamond. This diamond contains four points of blue. These points symbolize compassion toward yourself and others, receptivity to love, wisdom in your attractions, and sensitivity to your needs and those of others in an equal balance of giving and receiving.

Now move to the throat chakra. To visualize this energy center, see a pentagon with two yellow points in the middle and three blue points surrounding them. These points create a field of green, which symbolizes verbal creativity. Through positive thoughts and words, you create your experiences of learning, healing, prosperity, and expansion.

Proceed to the brow chakra, home of insight and intuition. As you breathe in, visualize a splendid six-pointed star. Each opposite point of the star contains one each of the three primary colors. In your mind's eye, see these colors merging into the color indigo. This indigo star helps you open the intuition, stimulate mental clarity, and bring wisdom to your thoughts. It is a vision of unity as you see your true position in the universe. You are an integral part of a unified whole.

You finally reach the crown chakra. As you gently breathe in, visualize this chakra as a clear quartz crystal with all seven colors of the rainbow emanating from it. The crystal also radiates a yellow glow of both joy and understanding of your soul's union and purpose.

Chapter Four:
Christian Meditations

A Simple Christian Meditation

This meditation is designed to help make direct contact with
our deepest religious beliefs in a safe, quiet setting.

1. Perform one of the Basic Relaxation Exercises,
then recite the Lord's Prayer or another prayer of your
choice that has a special meaning to you.

*Our Father, who art in heaven, hallowed be thy name; thy kingdom
come; thy will be done on Earth as it is in heaven. Give us this day our daily*

bread; and forgive us our trespasses as we forgive those who trespass against us; and lead us not into temptation, but deliver us from evil. For thine is the kingdom, and the power, and the glory forever. Amen.

2. As you breathe, visualize the presence of God both within you and all around you.

3. Next, focus your mind and heart on a specific word or name that you relate to strongly, such as Christ, love, Mary, or holy. Repeat this word like a mantra and, while you breathe, use one repetition per outward breath. Feel the essence of this word or name permeate your entire being.

4. After several minutes, conclude your meditation. Express your gratitude at this time, if you wish.

The Centering Prayer Meditation

This exercise is based on the meditative practice of an early Christian monk. Mystics have described this exercise as "leading us to the heart of God." Its major purpose is to express our innate desire to know God, the Great Spirit, or Absolute Truth.

1. Begin this meditation by sitting on the floor or in a straight-backed chair with your eyes closed, being aware of your breathing. Work with your breath for several minutes as you slowly relax.

2. Imagine that you are sitting in the sky, above a

cloud. This is the "cloud of forgetting," to which you will send all of your body tensions, and all the worries of the day. Continue to do this until you feel totally relaxed. Continue breathing with awareness.

3. Now imagine another cloud above you, which is the "cloud of unknowing." In your mind's eye, imagine this cloud interpenetrating your entire being, including your body, thoughts, feelings, and spirit.

4. Remind yourself that you are seeking the truth and that your knowledge is limited at this time. Allow yourself to connect with the place within that is yearning to know the truth or the answer to a question that has eluded you up to now.

5. Allow this feeling to blend with your desire to connect with the Great Spirit, or God, where you will find the answer to your question.

6. Gently vocalize a word or short phrase that has religious significance for you. This may be a mantra, the name of a saint, or a phrase as simple as "God," "love," or "shalom." Repeat this word or phrase gently, but with deep feeling, as if it were the key to open the door to truth.

7. Allow your yearning to penetrate the cloud of unknowing that lies between yourself and the Great Spirit. Continue paying attention to your breathing, as you repeat your prayer or mantra.

8. Whenever something comes to mind, whether

a childhood hurt, or a thought or feeling that causes disharmony, repeat your mantra or prayer and direct it into the cloud of forgetting.

9. Be aware of the possibility of receiving love and wisdom from the Great Spirit as you continue this prayerful meditation. Allow it to permeate your being, as you breathe.

10. When you intuitively feel that the time is right, slowly conclude your meditation with an expression of thanks.

When practiced regularly, this meditation can help you to connect to the essence of the Great Spirit and integrate it into your daily life.

Listening to the Divine

Few of us realize that spiritual help is, as a teacher once said, "no more than your next breath away." The following simple meditation is designed to help us come into contact with Divine Energy, whether or not we believe in a Universal God, or the "God within."

1. Practice one of the Basic Relaxation Exercises, then recite a short prayer of your choosing that you feel brings you into closer contact with the Divine.
You may choose something like the Lord's Prayer, or

a simple prayer like "I ask to be open to the presence of God in my life at this time."

2. As you watch your breathing, verbally express a word (or words) that reflect a specific spiritual quality or attribute that you want to more fully manifest in your life right now. Repeat this word or phrase aloud (and with feeling) several times, until you sense that it has become more integrated into your consciousness.

3. Now, in silence, contemplate the meaning and deeper ramifications of your chosen word or phrase. What does it mean to you? How can it manifest in your life? How will it change you in the future? If you find your mind wandering from the subject, repeat the word or phrase aloud again.

4. After several minutes, allow yourself to conclude your meditation. End your meditation session with a prayer of thanks, or one that encompasses your chosen word, such as "I pray that love can more fully permeate my life," or "I pray to be more aware of opportunities to be generous today."

Forgiveness Meditations

Forgiveness has always been considered one of the most spiritual acts of life, in part because it is not often easy to do. When we feel we have been injured by another person, many of us hold a grudge for days, weeks, months, or even a lifetime.

When this happens, we harden our hearts, which can make us lose contact with our innate loving and Divine Nature.

Meditation for Forgiving Another

The following meditation is designed to facilitate forgiveness. Until you have gained considerable experience in both meditation and your chosen spiritual practice, the person you wish to forgive should not be someone whom you feel has committed a major wrong against you, but rather a person with whom you have had a minor conflict like an argument or disagreement. As you practice this meditation regularly, you can deal with those you feel have hurt you more deeply.

1. Get comfortable. If you are sitting on a mat, cross your legs; if you are sitting on a comfortable straight-backed chair, place your feet flat on the floor. Your spine should be straight, your shoulders relaxed, and your eyes should be positioned straight ahead. Fold your hands lightly in your lap or place them, palms up, on your thighs.

2. Gently close your eyes. Be aware of your breathing, which should be from the diaphragm. Don't try to control your breathing, but be aware of its rhythm. Maintain awareness of your breath for a few moments.

3. Now, slowly scan your body, moving downward from the top of your head. Be aware of your head for a few moments, and then slowly extend your attention downward to your neck, chest, shoulders, arms, hands; your abdomen, lower back, pelvic area; and your thighs, legs, and feet. Wherever you feel tension, breathe into that area, visualizing relaxation and warmth reaching that part of your body. This process should take several minutes.

4. When your body is fully relaxed and aware of itself, bring your attention back to your breath for a few moments.

5. Now bring to mind someone whom you feel has wronged you recently, and whom you have not yet forgiven.

6. Review the unpleasant exchange or situation as it occurred, without exaggerating or otherwise altering any element.

7. Gently ask yourself the following questions:

∗ How might this exchange have occurred in a more positive way?

∗ What could I have said (or not said) or done (or not done) to have produced a different result?

∗ How might I have contributed to the problem due to feelings of pride, fear, or self-will?

∗ How might the other person have responded to any positive gestures on my part?

8. At this point, take a few deep breaths, and say aloud: "I wish to forgive, as I wish to be forgiven."

9. Allow yourself to feel compassion and forgiveness for the person, even if it is just a small amount of forgiveness at first (you can repeat this meditation whenever you wish).

10. Then take a few more deep breaths, slowly open your eyes, and return to everyday reality once more.

If you can, communicate with that person and offer your forgiveness. As a result of the meditation, you may also want to ask for forgiveness yourself, since you may have discovered that you contributed to the unpleasant situation.

If the other person refuses to communicate with you, try again another time. If the other person insists on holding a grudge against you, know that you have done your best and can get on with your life.

If the other person is no longer living, forgive him or her "in the spirit." You may wish to express your forgiveness in a more concrete way by visiting the gravesite or by donating money to a charity in the person's memory.

Self-Forgiveness Meditation

While forgiving other people is not always easy, forgiving ourselves is often more difficult. The following meditation is designed to help us cultivate self-forgiveness and begin to free ourselves of the limits that an unforgiving attitude imposes on our life.

1. Get comfortable. If you are sitting on a mat, cross your legs; if you are sitting on a comfortable straight-backed chair, place your feet flat on the floor. Your spine should be straight, your shoulders relaxed, and your eyes should be positioned straight ahead. Fold your hands lightly in your lap or place them, palms up, on your thighs.

2. As you watch your breathing, allow yourself to consider one aspect of your life that you truly regret. It may be something you did or said to another person, a limiting or negative attitude, or a lie of omission that you regret deeply.

3. Allow this memory to surface, without judging it or censoring it in any way. Be aware of your emotional and physical reactions as you continue to watch your breathing. Examine the issues behind the regret and see it as part of your life history.

4. Then ponder on how you can atone for this source of regret. Does it involve asking forgiveness from another person? Does it involve a radical change of attitude or belief? Does it involve a concrete act of redemption?

Also, ask yourself if you may be overreacting to the original situation. Have you been carrying a burden of guilt for too long? Might there be a different perspective that will allow you to move forward in your life? Allow your thoughts and feelings to come up and record them in a journal.

5. Ask for help in transcending this regret and making it into a stepping stone to help you reach a new level of being. Say a prayer like, "I pray to forgive myself."

6. As you conclude your meditation, take a few deep breaths and stretches before you get up.

Goodness Meditation

Many of us underestimate our gifts and do not acknowledge our good deeds and other accomplishments. While not intended as an ego trip, the following meditation helps us to take stock of the good things we have done in our lives.

1. Sit comfortably in a straight-backed chair or on a meditation mat. Perform one of the Basic Relaxation Exercises. Be aware of your breathing and take deep yet gentle breaths.

2. As you watch your breathing, pray, "I ask to acknowledge the good I have done in my life."

3. With pen in hand, begin to write down all the beautiful, loving things you have done in your life. These may include acts of compassion and generosity, right attitudes, or acts of courage: anything about which you feel particularly good (even if you might have forgotten it up to now). Be aware of any period in your life that was especially rich in good deeds and loving actions.

4. After several minutes of brainstorming, read the list over. Say to yourself, "I acknowledge the goodness within me." At this point, you may wish to express grati-

tude for your life and your innate gift of goodness.
Ask the Great Spirit for more opportunities to express
goodness in your life.

Meditations of Gratitude

Many of us experience feelings of melancholy from time to
time. We sometimes focus on our failings and highlight what
is missing, rather than acknowledging the positive aspects of
ourselves and what is good in our lives. While not encouraging us to seek an escape from our problems, the following
meditations are designed to help us come in contact with the
many positive aspects of our life at present and to feel gratitude for what we have.

I

1. Do one of the Basic Relaxation Exercises, then say
a simple prayer like, "I pray to be aware of what I am
grateful for in my life."

2. Pen and journal in hand, begin writing a list
of what you have to be grateful for. This list can include
aspects of your personality you are happy with, the presence of certain people in your life, your pet, certain
possessions you have, your job, knowledge or insights you
may have gained, your health, your favorite tree in your
front yard, and whatever else may come into your mind.

3. Do not censor the flow of ideas; simply allow your

active mind to brainstorm as you record your impressions in your journal. Allow several minutes for this exercise. When you are finished, read over each impression either silently or aloud.

4. When you have finished reading your list, devote a minute or so to quiet breathing. Conclude your meditation with a prayer of thanks.

II

1. Perform one of the Basic Relaxation Exercises, then, on a piece of paper, write the names of every person who has been kind to you, either today or during your lifetime. This may include people who have done you a special favor, listened to your troubles, helped you with a problem, given you a hug when you needed it, or who have performed an especially caring act that you have never been able to forget.

2. When you have finished, read their names, either singly or as a group, and say, "May (name) receive God's grace," "I thank God for having [name] in my life," or another expression of your choosing.

Angel Meditations

Whenever we go to sleep, our soul enters the subtle realms of existence where angelic forces reside. An important aspect of religious belief since ancient times, angels have long been considered God's messengers who offer us protection, guidance, and healing.

The following meditations, done as we are about to go to sleep at night, are designed to help us make contact with the angelic realms and open ourselves to their blessings during sleep.

I

1. While lying in bed, close your eyes and breathe deeply for several minutes. Visualize areas of tension in your body and allow them to relax one by one.

2. When you feel relaxed and in a receptive mood, recite a favorite prayer of your choice or chant a mantra that is especially meaningful to you, such as: "Oh, Powers of Love, I pray to commune with the Angels tonight." Continue your breathing with this feeling in your heart.

3. In your mind's eye, visualize an angelic being. It may be the type of angel you have seen in religious art, or the angel may take another form, such as a core of pure, white light. Imagine yourself communing with this angelic being, allowing the angel's energy to permeate your entire being. Feel the healing, the lightness, and the comfort that is enveloping you at this time. Continue to breathe and relax.

4. At this point, many people fall asleep. However, if you are still awake, allow your consciousness to bring up a problem that you have been having, or an issue that you have been having difficulty with, such as a health problem, a difficult decision that has been on your mind, or a concern you have for a friend or relative. Visualize the problem being offered to the angelic light. At this point, you can say, "I pray for assistance in resolving this problem in the light of God's will," or simply, "I pray for healing and wholeness."

5. Continue to breathe comfortable, deep breaths, and allow yourself to drift off to sleep.

When you awaken in the morning, you will feel alive and refreshed. You may also experience a feeling of reso-lution (or beginning resolution) regarding the problems you have been dealing with.

This feeling can easily be brought into your morning meditation as you continue a benign cycle of healing and blessings from the angelic realms.

II

1. While you are lying in bed, close your eyes and breathe deeply for several minutes. Visualize areas of ten-sion in your body and allow them to relax one by one.

2. Review the day's events in your mind. If anyone has wronged you in any way during the day, send them feelings of compassion and forgiveness. If you have wronged others, feel remorse for your actions, but be careful not to wallow in guilt. Affirm that you do not want to repeat this action, and pray to be more aware so you do not repeat it in the future. If you have hurt another person by your action, resolve to ask forgiveness of that person. Continue to breathe deeply.

3. Now visualize four angels above you, watching over you as you sleep. They represent four Divine Aspects that are with us always.

* On the right, feel the presence of the Archangel Michael, representing Divine Mercy, which forgives our mistakes.

* On the left, feel the presence of the Archangel Gabriel, representing Divine Strength, protecting us from worry and fear.

* Behind you, feel the fiery presence of the angel Uriel, representing Divine Light, illuminating our souls with wisdom and insight.

* In front of you, feel the presence of the Archangel Raphael, the angel of Healing, promoting integration and wholeness, as well as physical, emotional, and spiritual renewal.

4. Besides all four angels, strive to be conscious of the presence of God, who both includes and transcends these four Divine Aspects. At this point, you may wish to say a statement like, "God is One," "There is One God," or "Thank You, Great Spirit, and Your Holy Angels, for your blessings as I sleep." Repeat this until you fall asleep.

Guardian Angel Meditation

Some Western religions teach of the existence of guardian angels: one or more personal angels who guide us and protect us throughout our lives. In Exodus (23:20) Yahweh declares to Moses: "Behold, I send an Angel before thee, to keep thee in the way, and to bring thee into the place which I have prepared. Beware of him and obey his voice . . ."

Guardian angels have long been recognized as guides who help oversee the processes of our personal evolution, and offer us guidance, support, and comfort as we tread the often difficult path of living in the day-to-day world.

Invisible Helper Meditation

Whenever we go to sleep, our soul enters the subtle realms of existence where we can commune with angels or God's messengers. The theosophical teacher C.W. Leadbeater taught that many of us can work with angels when we are asleep and help them assist humans and other living forms that are in need. He believed that during natural disasters like floods or earthquakes, humans can assist angels in offering comfort, protection, and even practical guidance on a soul level and helping to relieve suffering. This assistance may be used only during natural disasters. As spiritual law teaches that like attracts like, we may be asked to serve compatible individuals literally anywhere in the world with any type of problem.

The following meditation, done as we are about to go to

sleep, is designed to help us make contact with the angelic realms and serve as invisible helpers while we are asleep.

1. While lying in your bed, close your eyes and breathe deeply for several minutes. Recite a favorite prayer, chant, or mantra that is especially meaningful to you. At this point you can simply ask, "Oh, Powers of Love, I pray to serve as an Invisible Helper tonight if it is God's Will."

2. At this point, you may feel compassion for those who were involved in a natural disaster or other mass tragedy, or you may feel the pain of a friend or relative who is experiencing suffering or grief. Let feelings of love and compassion well up in your heart and visually send the person your love and support. You may repeat either aloud or to yourself, "I pray to be of service to those who are suffering."

3. Continue to breathe comfortable, deep breaths, and allow yourself to drift off to sleep.

Some who ask to serve as invisible helpers may experience vivid dreams that reveal their experience during the hours of sleep. If you have such an experience, write it down or record it. Others simply wake up feeling as though they accomplished something important during the night, although they may not have any recollection of what actually occurred. If you are one of these, don't worry. It is not really important that you remember a good deed. The point is that you have offered to help alleviate suffering in the world and left the rest to the angels!

Meditation to Protect a Loved One

1. Perform Step 1 of the Invisible Helper Meditation. Say a prayer such as, "I pray for Divine protection for [name] today."

2. Envision white light filling the room.

3. Visualize the loved one being surrounded by this globe of shimmering white light. If your loved one is flying in an airplane, for example, visualize the light surrounding both the person and the aircraft. Know that your loved one is in God's hands and is completely safe. Con-tinue this visualization for several minutes, or until you feel comfortable about your loved one's welfare. If you wish to recite a prayer asking for protection, do so at this time.

4. As you conclude, say a brief prayer of thanks. Take several deep breaths and stretch for a few moments before rising.

Chapter Five: Healing Meditations

Healing Meditation

Meditation is a powerful tool for healing. As opposed to curing, healing is a process rather than a goal. It encompasses the entire spectrum of the human being—physical, emotional, mental, and spiritual.

Healing implies viewing our situation in a wider perspective, beyond the treatment of symptoms, that embraces all aspects of our lives. Rather than fixating on symptoms (which can distract us from the healing process), healing means learning from the crisis (the symptom) rather than trying to control or eliminate it. It means developing the flexibility needed to change attitudes that keep us out of touch with our innate intelligence, respect, and love.

Healing also involves enduring pain or discomfort while expanding our view to learn what the suffering has to teach us. Rather than trying to "fix" symptoms or pain from the outside (through therapeutic means, natural or otherwise), healing means taking responsibility for growth and change from the inside. Meditation can be a powerful tool to facilitate self-healing and inner growth.

Healing with Visualization

Creative visualization is often used in a healing meditation. Louise L. Hay, author of *You Can Heal Your Life,* gives three basic elements of a positive healing visualization, which we can adapt to our individual needs:

* An image of the problem or pain or disease, or the diseased part of the body
* An image of a positive force eliminating this problem
* An image of the body being rebuilt to perfect health, and then seeing the body move through life with ease and energy

Positive visualization can incorporate literal images, symbolic images related to treatment, or abstract images. A universal image is a bright, white healing light. Imagine it shining around (and through) every aspect of your being.

A powerful tool for this type of visualization meditation is "The Divine Light Invocation Mantra" taught by Swami Sivananda Radha:

I am created by Divine Light.
I am sustained by Divine Light.
I am protected by Divine Light.
I am surrounded by Divine Light.
I am ever growing into Divine Light.

Some people may wish to visualize being healed by Jesus Christ or the Healing Buddha, while others may wish to incorporate saints, yogis, angels, or other spiritual beings in their healing meditations.

Accessing Healing Guidance

Many believe that healing has to do with their physician's expertise or the medication given, overlooking the fact that it is our own body that is doing the work: healing is an inside job. A health professional can help initiate and maintain the healing process, but it is we ourselves who do the healing.

Since self-healing may involve personal issues such as childhood hurts, poor self-image, negative attitudes, wrong assumptions, and anger towards oneself, ones family, or friends, this meditation acts as a vehicle for self-exploration and self-discovery while embarking on a healing journey.

This simple meditation is designed to help us take greater

responsibility for our healing and access inner wisdom regarding our health situation. Repeat this daily meditation as often as you need.

1. Sit comfortably and do one of the Basic Relaxation Exercises. When you feel comfortable and relaxed, say clearly, slowly, and purposefully: "I am a self-healing being. I have an unlimited capacity to heal myself. I pray to access my body's innate healing power to the fullest." You may want to repeat this prayer several times so that it becomes more integrated into your consciousness.

2. Devote several minutes to receptive silence. Chances are that many thoughts and feelings will come, including fear, anger, frustration, doubt, and judgments; you may have feelings of resistance to healing, or even a desire to remain sick. By the same token, you may experience inspiration and lightness, along with a feeling that you are open to new ideas and possibilities; some may involve practical guidance that can facilitate your healing and assist your health practitioner in helping you. Allow these thoughts and feelings to surface, without judging or censoring them.

3. Write your impressions in a notebook. Some of these ideas or impressions may be subjects of meditation themselves.

4. When you feel ready to end your meditation, take several deep breaths before slowly getting up.

Accessing Deeper Healing Wisdom

This meditation is similar to Accessing Healing Guidance, but is intended to be used by those who have already done some exploration with that meditation.

Many of us feel victimized when we are ill or have suffered an accident, and are eager to have unpleasant symptoms relieved as soon as possible. Yet we can also use our pain and suffering as a springboard to learn more about ourselves and to develop new goals and areas of interest. This meditation allows us to move deeper into the healing process, and to work with specific issues that may have come to our attention.

1. Sit comfortably in a straight-backed chair or on a meditation mat. Do one of the Basic Relaxation Exercises. When you feel comfortable and relaxed, say clearly, slowly, and purposefully: "I pray to discover the inner meanings of my health problem." You may want to repeat this prayer several times so that it becomes more integrated into your consciousness.

2. As you breathe quietly and evenly, allow yourself to ponder your prayer request. Rather than feel victimized by your health problem, ask if there might be a pattern or rhythm to your symptoms, especially if you have suffered a similar health problem previously. Is your health problem offering you any opportunities for personal growth? Are there any positive components to your health problem, such as time off from work, greater self-nurturing, or changes in your thinking and goals? What new insights have you gained about your life and relationships? What would you like to change about your life, if you could? Are there any areas of interest you would like to pursue? Allow your responses to surface, without judging or censoring them. Write your impressions in a notebook.

3. When you feel ready to end your meditation, take several deep breaths before slowly getting up.

As with the previous exercise, repeat this daily meditation as often as you need.

Healing Light Meditation

This powerful meditation is designed to enable you to access the powers of healing in the universe.

1. Sit comfortably either in a straight-backed chair or on a cushion or mat. Once in a comfortable posture, do one of the Basic Relaxation Exercises.

2. As you sit quietly with your hands folded on your lap, visualize a tiny point of pure, white light located about six inches (fifteen centimeters) above your head.

3. Visualize this light getting brighter. As it brightens, it sends out strong beams of light just in front of you, to your right, to your left, and behind you. You see yourself surrounded by brilliant white light on all sides. It makes you feel secure and blessed.

4. As you continue to be aware of your breathing, inhale this light through your nose. Feel the light entering your lungs and penetrating every part of your body. Feel its healing power. Feel its wisdom.

5. Now, visualize a blue light beginning to move through your body, exiting through the soles of your feet. This is a cleansing light, and it is sweeping away any negative thoughts, inner disharmony, pain, and tension that you may have been holding. Breathe in the white light, and exhale the blue light, knowing that you are being healed by the incoming "white" breath and cleansed by the outgoing "blue" breath.

6. Continue this exercise for several minutes. As you slowly come out of your meditation, visualize the light fading until it again becomes the tiny point of light above your head. Express gratitude to the light, and ask that it remain with you throughout the day. Know, too, that you can access its power at any time.

Meditation for Managing Pain

1. Sit comfortably either in a straight-backed chair or on a cushion or mat. Once in a comfortable posture, do one of the Basic Relaxation Exercises.

2. Remember an event or experience that you

thoroughly enjoyed. It may be a time that made you happy, a special meal, or an experience with a special person you remember with fondness. Recall the details of that experience, including sights, sounds, colors, and tastes. Recall the feelings that you had, and savor the memories.

3. Now, move your visualization to another event, such as a celebration. Recall the laughter, the play, the feelings of happiness you had. Savor your memory of the experience, and bring it into the present moment.

4. Visualize some of your accomplishments in life, or aspects of your life that are special sources of pride and happiness for you. Allow yourself to feel good about yourself and your accomplishments.

5. Continue to be aware of your breathing. Visualize these good feelings flowing into the area of your body that is in pain. Feel their warmth and healing power. Know that these memories and experiences are parts of your total being-your living history.

6. Slowly conclude your meditation. Take several deep breaths, stretch, and slowly rise from your meditation posture.

Inner Wisdom Healing Meditation

This meditation helps us come in contact with our body's inner wisdom; the ultimate source of healing.

1. Sit comfortably either in a straight-backed chair or on a cushion or mat. Once in a comfortable posture, do one of the Basic Relaxation Exercises.

2. As you take full, deep, and easy breaths, feel your body relaxing totally. At the same time, feel the aliveness of your body: Your energy is flowing, your emotions are stable, and your mind is alert.

3. Perform a "mental scan" of your body. Be aware of the myriad activities of circulation, digestion, elimination, temperature regulation, and protection that your brain, nervous system, immune system, muscles, and organs are doing on their own, without you even having to think about them. Feel your body's ability to maintain and heal itself.

4. Allow yourself to experience a sense of gratitude and wonder. Tell your body that you are grateful.

5. Now, ask your body what it needs at this time to facilitate healing. You may need to ask more than once. Be open to receiving any answer that may come up; it may involve proper nutrition, rest, exercise, therapeutic procedures, herbs, or something else. Write your impressions in a journal.

Yogananda Healing Meditation

This healing meditation technique is based on one introduced by Paramahansa Yogananda, the respected Indian teacher and author of the acclaimed book Autobiography of a Yogi. It is primarily intended to enable you to help heal someone else.

1. Sit upright in a comfortable, straight-backed chair.

2. Focus your attention on the "spiritual eye," which is the area between your eyebrows. It is also the "will power" center of the body.

3. After several minutes, think of the spiritual eye of the person you wish to send healing energy to (holding a photograph of this person in front of you may help you to visualize better).

4. Don't think of the person's disease, but think instead of the healing process that is strengthening the innate healing power of the person.

5. Visualize healing light moving through your medulla oblongata at the base of your brain; then draw that healing light through the point between your eyebrows. Send the healing light through this center into the spiritual eye of the person you wish to help.

6. Devote several minutes to filling the person's whole body with healing light.

7. Recite the following affirmation:
O Infinite Spirit
Thou art omnipotent.
Thou art in all thy children.
Thou art in (name of the person to be healed).

Manifest Thy heavenly presence in his/her
body, mind, and soul.

8. Rub your hands together briskly until you feel a
magnetic charge in them; this will probably manifest as a
warm, tingling sensation. Hold your hands up, palms out,
to send the healing energy to the recipient.

9. Chant Aum three times.

10. As you continue to hold up your hands, move
them up and down in space.

11. Visualize sending the energy as long as you feel
inspired to do so.

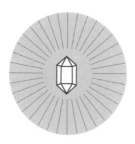

Chapter Six: Nature Meditations

Nature is a powerful source of beauty and inspiration, and meditating in a natural setting can be an unforgettable experience. However, even if we cannot meditate in a natural setting, we can create a visualization of nature in our minds. The following meditations are devoted to exploring our connection with the natural world, and using its magic to facilitate inner healing and transformation.

A Meditation in Nature

Being in nature helps mobilize our five basic senses and stimulates our sixth sense-intuition. When going into nature to meditate, choose a natural form that attracts you, such as a lake, stream, (or some other body of water), tree, flower, cliff, meadow, or mountain. Using your senses of sight, hearing, smell, touch, and (if appropriate) taste, "observe" the natural form. Breathe fully, but without forcing your breath.

Close your eyes, but continue to visualize the natural form in your mind's eye. As you breathe, be aware of any thoughts, feelings, memories, or personal associations that might come up. Be especially aware of your feelings, without judging them.

Slowly open your eyes and come out of your meditation. Devote several minutes to recording your impressions in a journal. Conclude by giving thanks to the natural form that assisted you in your meditation practice.

The following meditations can be done indoors.

In the Apple Orchard

1. Sit comfortably in a straight-backed chair or on a meditation mat on the floor. Be aware of your breathing. Do one of the Basic Relaxation Exercises.

2. After you have relaxed your body and mind, imagine yourself walking down a path toward an apple orchard.

3. Visualize the trees in the orchard bearing the ripest of fruit. Bees, butterflies, and songbirds are everywhere. In the distance, you hear a rushing stream. Pause for a moment and listen to it.

4. Feel yourself being welcomed into the orchard by the bees, birds, and the trees themselves. It's a magical feeling. Pause.

5. Imagine yourself bowing in honor of one of the trees, and express the greeting, "Your life is one with mine." Pause.

6. Picture yourself picking an apple from the tree. Bring it to your chest and hold it up in front of you. Pause.

7. Imagine yourself biting into the apple. It is the most delicious and juicy apple you have ever tasted. Imagine the apple's essence awakening your taste buds and then permeating your entire being, bringing you nourishment, cleansing, and inner healing.

8. After several minutes, respectfully take leave of the orchard, and return to your normal state of consciousness. Take several deep breaths and stretch, if you like. Slowly leave your sitting position.

By the River

1. As in the previous meditation, sit comfortably in a straight-backed chair or on a meditation mat on the floor. Do one of the Basic Relaxation Exercises. Be aware of your breathing.

2. After you have relaxed your body and mind, place your focus on your heart. It is constantly pumping blood throughout your body, and is also the abode of your love.

3. Visualize your heart as a river of pure, clean water. On the shore of the river is an altar made up entirely of precious stones, including amethysts, emeralds, rubies, and diamonds. Behind the altar are lush, tropical trees in full blossom. The blossoms are beautiful to behold and their aroma permeates all of your senses.

4. Visualize yourself seated within this beautiful scene, feeling one with it. Your heart feels rich and expansive. It is the center of your life. Enjoy your visit here. Express gratitude to be able to enjoy such richness in your life.

5. After several minutes, respectfully take your leave, and return to your normal state of consciousness. Take several deep breaths and stretch, if you like. Slowly leave your sitting position.

Four Elements Meditation

The purpose of these meditations is to allow us to deepen our connection with the four elements: Earth, Fire, Water, and Air. These meditations are most successful when done outdoors in a natural setting, but that is not essential.

Earth

As you sit comfortably on a straight-backed chair or lie down on your back, devote several minutes to progressive relaxation, using one of the Basic Relaxation Exercises. Pay special attention to your breathing. Visualize all the tension leaving your body until you feel completely relaxed.

Feel your physical and energetic connection to the Earth. Imagine that its strength is not only supporting you, but is giving you vital energy. Remember that the Earth contains minerals, like iron, calcium, silica, and magnesium that are also found in your body, so you have both an energetic and biochemical connection to our planet. Feel this connection and your gratitude toward the Earth element as you continue to breathe deeply.

Fire

This meditation is best done on a sunny day (wear a hat or sunscreen as needed).

Sit comfortably on a straight-backed chair or lie down on your back. Devote several minutes to progressive relaxation. Take full, deep breaths, knowing that you are bringing the life force into your body with each incoming breath.

Feel the warmth and light of the Sun on your body. The fire of the Sun can destroy, but it is essential for life and cre-ation. As you breathe, focus on the essential qualities of life: heat, passion, purification. Feel the heat within your body, filling you with passion and inspiration. Know too that the Fire element in your body allows your immune system to function, killing viruses, bacteria, and germs with the purify-ing heat. Feel the Fire within fill you with the energy to develop creative visions and achieve new goals. Feel your gratitude for the Fire element in your life.

Water

Sit or lie down near a river, lake, or some other body of water. If this is not possible, sit near a fountain. A glass of water will even do.

Devote several minutes to progressive relaxation and deep breathing until you feel completely relaxed.

Visualize the element of Water and the importance it has in your life. Ponder its nourishing and purifying qualities. Think about the spiritual essence of water and flowing water as symbolizing the movement of life. Remind yourself that over 75 percent of your body is made up of water, and imagine how water functions in your organs, tissues, and body processes, like circulation, locomotion, elimination, and digestion. Visualize the Water element bringing you cleansing and healing, and feel your gratitude toward it.

Air

This meditation is best done outdoors. Sit comfortably on a straight-backed chair or on the ground. Devote several minutes to deep, rhythmic breathing, as in one of the Breathing Exercises. Continue to practice deep breathing until you feel completely relaxed.

Focus your attention on the all-pervading qualities of

Air: the air that you breathe and that gives you the gift of life; the gentle breezes that caress your face, and the winds that bring new ideas and fresh perspectives. Feel your connection with the Air element within-the oxygen that energizes and nourishes every cell of your body. As you breathe deeply of the life-giving Air, feel your gratitude towards it.

Flower Meditation

In addition to their beauty, flowers are potent sources of inspiration and wisdom. They elevate our spirits, and bring us hope and comfort during times of difficulty. Many feel that the presence of flowers in a hospital room can help speed the patient's recovery considerably.

Meditating with flowers can be a powerful experience that is both gentle and transformational. The following four meditations utilize the power of flowers in different ways. You can vary the first three meditations with different flowers, which imparts a different quality to each meditative experience.

I

Place a single flower in a vase and set it before you. If you do not have access to a fresh flower, a color photograph of a flower will do.

1. Perform one of the Basic Relaxation Exercises.
2. Observe the flower carefully: its colors, textures,

aroma, and form. After a few minutes of observation, gently close your eyes, seeing the flower in your mind's eye.

3. Think about what the flower means to you, both as a symbol and as a friend. As you observe your thoughts about the flower, be aware of other associations that may come to mind.

4. As the mental images of the flower begin to fade, open your eyes again. After a few minutes of observation, gently conclude your meditation.

II

Pen and notebook in hand, go outdoors and quietly observe the flowers in your garden or neighborhood. Take your time and observe them as though doing a walking meditation. Chances are that you will be intuitively drawn to one flower in particular; you may even feel that the flower itself is trying to attract your attention!

Quietly observe the flower. Carefully observe its form, color, aroma, and "energetic presence" in the garden. If you wish, gently touch the flower. Send the flower your good feelings. As another living being, the flower responds to your energy the same way you respond to the flower. Devote several minutes to quiet observation.

Sitting on the ground (if possible), perform one of the Basic Relaxation Exercises. At this point, you can silently contemplate the flower with your eyes open. Or, if you choose, you can mentally ask the flower for a message that resonates with your idea of the flower's essential "keynote quality," such as enthusiasm, delicacy, flexibility, or strength. Very often, you may receive a mental impression from the flower concerning a matter of importance, or you can ask, "Please teach me about healing," or "Please teach me about beauty." It may be a message you can write down in your notebook, or you may wish to draw the flower instead. Be calm and open to any eventuality. Devote a maximum of ten minutes to this meditation exercise, especially at first.

III

A Healing Meditation with Flowers

1. Go to a garden or to some wild flowers in a field. It is important that you allow yourself to be drawn to the specific flowers you wish to work with today. Sit comfortably on the ground. Devote several minutes to one of the Basic Relaxation Exercises, until you feel comfortable and relaxed.

2. Silently observe the flowers. As you contemplate them, visualize their beginning from a tiny seed deep in the Earth. Imagine them breaking through the soil. Observe the flower's color, form, and overall beauty. Feel its strength and vitality, its utter joy to be alive, and its ability to express itself to the fullest—even in a difficult environment. Allow yourself to connect with the energy of the flower.

3. Take several deep breaths. Turn your focus back to yourself and your own physical and emotional condition. Note that both you and the flowers share the same life force that comes from the Earth, which assures your survival, growth, and healing, and that the possibilities for healing are tremendous.

4. Offer a prayer such as, "I pray for the power of nature to help me heal my life," or create one that applies more to your specific health situation. Allow yourself to feel inspiration and appreciation for the beauty around you.

5. Before concluding your meditation, take several deep breaths and stretch.

IV

Red Rose Meditation

The red rose is a powerful symbol of human love. Among the most valued of garden flowers, the rose is an enduring symbol of unfolding love. This meditation is related to the chakra meditations discussed elsewhere in this book; refer to the section discussing chakra meditations on page 64 before you do this one.

1. Sit comfortably in a straight-backed chair or on a meditation cushion or mat. Be aware of your breathing. Take slow, deep, and even breaths. At each exhalation, feel the tension drain out of your body and mind.

2. When you feel fully relaxed, visualize your heart chakra as a pure, fresh rosebud ready to open.

3. Continue your breathing. Visualize the rosebud opening slowly. As it unfolds, pay attention to each individual petal as representing a quality of love. These may include compassion, caring, devotion, protection, passion, kindness, selflessness, service, caring, and nurturing.

4. As your heart center continues to open, think of those you love and send them love at this time. As the rose opens, imagine these feelings of love radiating outward into the world. Don't forget to include yourself as well. Allow at least several minutes for this part of the meditation.

5. As you continue to breathe, allow your heart feelings to expand their range so that you are radiating love to the larger community. See your heart as full and healthy, radiating love and light.

6. As you conclude your meditation, take several deep breaths, holding your hands to your heart center. After a few stretches, slowly get up from your meditation position.

Tree Meditation

Trees have always played a central role in the survival of

humanity and in the flowering of myriad cultures, including the ancient Egyptian, Hebrew, Greek, Roman, Indian, Japanese, Chinese, and Native American. Although many of us consider trees to be inanimate objects, native peoples have long considered them sacred beings offering wisdom, guidance, inspiration, and healing. Many believe that because humans and trees both live in the vertical dimension (although trees remain in one place throughout their lives while humans are constantly moving), we share a special bond of friendship. The following meditations are designed to help us create a deeper connection with trees and open ourselves to their life-giving and life-affirming nature.

Receiving Guidance

Pen and notebook in hand, go outdoors and quietly observe the trees in a park or forest. Take your time and observe the trees as though you were doing one of the walking meditations in this book. Chances are that you will be intuitively drawn to one tree in particular; as with the flower meditation, you may even feel that the tree itself it trying to attract your attention.

Quietly observe the tree at first, and then move slowly toward it. Carefully observe its form, leaves, and colors; be aware also of its "energetic presence." Silently extend a friendly greeting to the tree, as you would when you meet a new human friend. As another living being, the tree will respond to your energy the same way you respond to it. Touch the trunk, the branches, and leaves, if you wish; get to know the tree as another living being. Remember that humans and trees are chemically and biologically connected, since, in addition to providing us with food and medicine, trees provide us with the oxygen we need to survive. Express your gratitude to the tree for its gifts to humanity. Devote several minutes in quiet observation and communion.

Sitting comfortably on the ground (or on a bench if one is handy), perform one of the Basic Relaxation Exercises described earlier. Silently contemplate the tree with your eyes open for a few minutes. At this point, you can make a choice regarding the direction of your meditation:

1. Holding the image of the tree in your consciousness, you can close your eyes and meditate silently for five to ten minutes. If your mind begins to wander, open your eyes and refresh your image of the tree. Be aware of your breathing and of any thoughts or feelings that come up regarding the tree and your relationship to it.

2. You can mentally ask the tree for a message. You may have a question or problem that you have difficulty with or you can simply ask the tree for help in general. Record your impressions in a journal. Be calm and open for any eventuality.

3. Devote a maximum of ten minutes to this meditation, especially at first. If you feel a special connection with the tree, return for additional meditation sessions.

4. Conclude your meditation with a brief expression of gratitude. Do several stretches and slowly rise from your meditation posture.

Meditations on Individual Tree Species

1. Go to a tree or imagine yourself standing near a tree.

2. Stand comfortably erect, making sure your knees are not locked. Feel your feet on the ground and the ground supporting your body.

3. Imagine a vertical line in the center of your being moving down from the sky through your spine, and continuing through both feet, penetrating the Earth.

4. Breathe normally, with an awareness of your breath.

5. Try to "feel" what it is like to be a tree (devote at least two minutes to each of the following exercises):

Oak Meditation Feel your body strong and straight. Hold your arms open, palms up. Feel yourself stable against the winds of life, while flexible and able to adapt to challenges. Affirm your groundedness in truth. Visualize providing others with nourishment, strength, and protection. Feel your connection to both the Earth and the sky, drawing both wisdom from the Earth and nourishment from the sky and Sun.

Pine Meditation Feel your body strong and straight. Imagine your head to be higher than it actually is. Hold your arms open at a 45-degree angle to your body, palms facing down. Feel your connection to the Earth. Feel yourself solid yet flexible, with your boughs offering a blessing to those around you. Meditate on the concept of compassion and see yourself as a source of understanding and compassion for others.

Gingko Meditation Feel yourself as ancient as the Earth itself, going back to the time of the dinosaurs, unique and unconventional. As an aged being from the East, acknowledge your ability to adapt and thrive, even in difficult circumstances. Specifically acknowledge how you have succeeded in your life up to now, and how you have persevered. What innate talents and abilities did you use to accomplish this? See yourself as having succeeded while keeping your beauty and maintaining your individuality. Finally, acknowledge that your challenges in life are gifts from the Earth Mother that have strengthened you and increased your power and resourcefulness.

Maple Meditation Feel yourself as abundant and receptive, with your branches opening in all directions, reaching out to others. Imagine your branches as a form of antennae, receiving information from the world around you. At the same time, be conscious of how you affect others around you through your thoughts, feelings, and actions. Visualize yourself receiving the best from others and giving your best in return. Finally, experience the joy of the maple tree: strong, bright, and intimately involved with life around it.

Weeping Willow Meditation Stand erect, with your shoulders relaxed and your arms at your sides. Visualize yourself as a tree of calm and grace, even when you are experiencing difficulty in your life. You are grounded in reality and acknowledge the truth of your situation at the moment. Now feel your strong connection to the Water element with its inherent fluidity and nourishing properties, giving life to every cell of your body. Acknowledge the Water element as a part of you that is ever present; at the same time, see yourself as part of this eternal movement of life.

Acorn Meditation After performing one of the Basic Relaxation Exercises, take an actual acorn and hold it in your hand; if an acorn is not available, use a photograph or hold a mental image of an acorn in your mind's eye.

As you hold or imagine it, allow your mind to explore any associations the acorn has for you. Continue to be aware of your breathing. If your mind moves too far afield from your subject, gently move your focus back to the image of the acorn. After several minutes, conclude your meditation.

A Healing Tree Meditation

Choose a large, healthy tree to which you feel drawn. Sit down either facing the tree, with your spine resting against it, or lie down with your feet touching (or almost touching) the tree. If you need support, or if you feel a special physical connection to the tree, embrace the tree with your body pressed against it.

1. Devote several minutes to one of the Basic Relaxation Exercises, until you feel comfortable and relaxed.

2. As you breathe evenly and fully, feel your energetic connection with the tree. Like the tree, imagine yourself to be in total alignment in your body, mind, and emotions. Feel the energy of the tree intermingling with yours. Feel the vital power of the tree strengthen your energy field and your feeling of being "grounded" in the Earth.

3. Ask the tree for healing. You can say something like, "Brother/sister tree, my life force is one with yours. Please help me to heal." Say this with feeling and sincerity, as though the tree is a dear friend who can truly assist you in the healing process.

4. Devote several minutes to receptive silence and contemplation. Allow yourself to be open to new (and possibly unexpected) ideas, impressions, and insights about your health situation and how you might improve it. Continue to breathe, taking slow, natural breaths, and feeling your connection to the tree and its indwelling spirit of intelligence, love, and power. Record your experiences in a journal, if you wish.

5. After ten minutes, you are ready to conclude your meditation. Express your gratitude to the tree and slowly take your leave. If you feel that you have benefited from this meditation, return to the tree again for additional healing sessions.

Water Meditations

One of these water meditations should be done outdoors, while the other can be done in the home.

I

Sit near a lake, stream, river, or ocean.

As you breathe quietly and evenly, observe the light reflecting on the water and see how it is constantly changing. Observe the changing light. As you do, see your mind alive and changing as well.

II

Place a glass of water in front of you.

As you breathe, observe the water as essential to your life. Observe your mind as you explore the meaning that water has for you. If your mind wanders, gently and patiently bring your focus back to the water. This part of the meditation can take several minutes.

As you continue your meditation, gently lift the glass and slowly drink the water, taking small sips at a time. Devote several minutes to ingesting the water. Be aware of any feelings as you do this.

Color Meditation

Color is a form of vibrational energy that can affect the way we think and feel: colors can depress us, or enable us to feel more optimistic; they can even help stimulate the immune system by their subtle influence on the human mind. We all know that walking into a room painted robin's-egg blue, for example, will produce a different feeling from a walking into a room painted bright red. By using color consciously, we can help bring about major changes in all areas of our lives.

The following meditations help us access the hidden powers of color and the power that they can bring to our lives on physical, psychological, and spiritual levels.

After performing one of the Basic Relaxation Exercises, visualize a field of color. You may also see the color as a flower, a light, a cloth, or a flame, such as a red rose, a blue sky, or a bright yellow sun. Visualize the color penetrating your entire being. In your mind's eye, feel the power that the particular color brings to your life, and how it can enhance your present-day reality.

Red ✱ arouses passion and desire. It is a color that is helpful to visualize when your energy level is low, or when you're lacking courage or motivation. Red can help you to feel your connection to nature. It also helps stimulate masculine energy and enables you to connect with qualities like strength, activity, assertiveness, protection, stability, realism, and objectivity.

Orange ✱ mobilizes your courage to try something new. It enhances your desire for forward movement and overcoming obstacles. Orange also helps you to become more open to your feelings and energizes psychic vision.

Yellow ✱ has long been linked with stimulating intellectual activity and increasing mental capacity, and for this reason is a good color to meditate on when you have research to do or an important decision to make. The color yellow rekindles dormant creativity and helps you feel more open to joy and humor. Drawing upon yellow also facilitates communication and helps you to become aware of new ideas.

Green ✱ is the color of healing and renewal. It enhances the desire for self-development and personal expansion, and facilitates getting in touch with your innate optimism and enthusiasm. Meditate on green when you feel that your health needs improvement or that you need to find a new direction in life.

Blue ✱ is viewed as a "quiet" color, which facilitates receptivity and relaxation. It helps you to surrender and access inner peace. The color blue also allows you to better feel your connection to celestial realms and stimulates your feminine qualities, such as sensitivity and intuitive recognition.

Indigo ✳ arouses the life force within (known as Kundalini)
and helps you to integrate your sexuality with spirituality.
Long connected to helping people become committed to a spiritual path (as well as embrace spiritual values in general), the
color indigo inspires you to realize your inner divinity. Meditate
on indigo if you want to find your spiritual direction in life.

Violet ✳ awakens inner devotion and enhances your perceptions
of universality and universal consciousness. It inspires soul-mate
recognition and helps you develop deeper psychic and spiritual
connections with loved ones. Violet is a healing color. It also
helps you to learn forgiveness, so it is a good color to meditate
on if you are angry or annoyed with yourself or anyone else.

White ✳ is not technically a color, but it is composed of all seven
colors of the rainbow. Meditating on white helps you perceive the
universality of people and things and enables you to view life
from a perspective of wholeness. At the same time, white awakens innocence and purity.

Rainbow Meditation

When you perform this meditation, imagine yourself sitting
underneath a rainbow's shining bands of color. Focus on
each color, one by one, and ponder the meaning it has in
your life.

Rainbow colors can also be seen to resonate with the different energy centers (chakras) of the body (see Chakra

Meditations page 64). Visualize each color around the corresponding chakra and think about what it means in that area of your life.

Red * root chakra

Orange * sacral chakra

Yellow * solar plexus chakra

Green * heart chakra

Blue * throat chakra

Indigo * brow chakra

Violet * crown chakra

After several minutes, visualize these different colors vibrating in harmony with each other throughout your body. Gradually see the colors blend until they merge to become a field of pure, white light. Feel the energy of this white light permeate your entire body ("As seven colored rays merge in white light"–Upanishads). Feel the power, perceptiveness, and inner healing that these wonderful combined energies provide. Gradually conclude your meditation with several deep breaths and stretches.

Walking Meditations

Most people believe that meditation is best practiced sitting on a straight-backed chair, cushion or mat. Yet walking meditation can trace its roots back hundreds of years to the Zen tradition. Like sitting meditations, walking meditations help the meditator to be aware. Yet unlike sitting, walking offers us a constant stream of images and experience that require constant observation.

Indoor Walking Meditation

For this meditation, you'll want to create a clear path at least twelve feet long. It's best to remove your shoes for this exercise so you can be in better contact with the floor.

1. Stand and devote several minutes to one of the Basic Relaxation Exercises. When your body is relaxed, bend your knees slightly and "feel" your feet connected to the floor. Place your hands gently at your sides, or clasp your hands behind your back. Remain conscious of your breathing.

2. Begin walking slowly, looking at the floor several feet ahead of you. Be aware of the forward movement of your body, as well as the connection of each foot touching the floor. Your mind will continually shift its focus as you apply your foot to the floor, place your weight on your foot, bend your knee, and move your other foot. Simply stay aware of your movement, which should be gradual, fluid, and easy.

3. When you reach the end of your indoor path, gently turn around. Be aware of your movements as you do this. Continue to observe your breathing, and be aware of any thoughts that come up. If you find yourself day-dreaming or being otherwise distracted, gently bring your focus back to your movement.

4. When you are ready to conclude your walking meditation, stand still for several minutes. Bend your knees slightly and be aware of your breathing, noting your inner calm and dignity.

Outdoor Walking Meditation (Alone)

For this walking meditation, you will either want to go bare-foot or wear light shoes or sandals. Choose a predetermined route that will be approximately twelve to twenty-seven feet (four to nine meters) in length.

1. Stand comfortably with your knees slightly bent, take a few moments to relax. As you watch your breathing, feel your feet firmly planted on the Earth.

2. Begin walking slowly, looking down several feet ahead of you. Be aware of your foot as it touches the ground. Feel the living Earth supporting your body as it moves.

3. When you reach the end of your path, stop; then turn around slowly. Remain mindful of your movement, as well as your connection to the Earth. Slowly return to your starting point, being mindful of your breathing, your movement, and your connection to the earth.

4. When you return to your starting point, stand still for several minutes, knees slightly bent. Continue to be aware of your breathing, as well as the supporting earth beneath your feet. As in the previous indoor walking meditation, note your feelings of inner calm and dignity.

Outdoor Walking Meditation (Accompanied)

This walking meditation requires a partner and a blindfold. Your partner will gently lead you, blindfolded, for a short walk on a route that you have both determined is safe.

1. Before you begin, devote several minutes to one of the Basic Relaxation Exercises described earlier. As in the previous walking meditation, bend your knees slightly and feel your connection to the earth, which is supporting you totally.

2. Put on the blindfold and have your partner turn you around several times so that you lose your sense of direction. Take your partner by the arm and have him/her silently lead you on a slow, yet steady walk.

3. As the two of you walk in silence, be aware of your feelings and sensations, without censoring them in any way. If you feel fear, observe it and, as you walk, "breathe into the fear" (the areas of your body where you experience it). Notice, too, any feelings of enjoyment, trust, and surrender.

4. Devote several minutes to this walking meditation. After you return to your original starting point, stand quietly for several minutes, being aware of your breathing as well as any feelings that come up.

5. After concluding your meditation, write your impressions in a journal or share your experience with your partner. Allow your partner to share his/her experiences with you as well.

Seeing and Listening

We often go through life in a state of non-attention. In order to function more efficiently in today's modern world, we often block out sights and sounds we don't wish to deal with. As a result, we may isolate ourselves from the rhythms of life and limit our life experience.

Seeing This simple meditation helps us cultivate the art of seeing. Leave your home for a walk through your neighborhood; devote from thirty to sixty minutes to this meditation so that you don't feel rushed. You may decide to choose the same route as you might take on an ordinary day, but this time you will walk slowly (at about half your normal speed) while paying close attention to everything in your range of vision.

In this walking meditation, you may wish to stop and observe a neighborhood tree, gaze at a flower by the roadside, or examine the shingles on the roof of a nearby house.

You may pause to watch children playing, or silently observe shoppers as they enter and leave the supermarket. Simply allow these sights to enter your consciousness without censoring or judging them in any way.

Continue walking. Chances are that you will see many familiar things, but will view them from a refreshingly new perspective.

Listening As you did in the previous meditation, walk in silence for thirty minutes to an hour. This may involve a walk in your neighborhood, in the park, or by the seashore. In this exercise, you are not to speak, but merely to listen, so you may want to limit your interaction with others. Listen to the sounds of nature, traffic, music, people talking, construction sounds, and the sounds of airplanes flying overhead. Try not to censor or block out any sounds. If any sounds distress you, breathe deeply to regain your composure.

Calling to Gaia: the Earth Goddess

Take a walking meditation in nature. Be especially aware of your breathing as you walk slowly in a natural setting, on a hiking trail, in a meadow, or by the seashore. Be especially aware of how you breathe and how and where you place your feet. Be receptive to the world around you, including the sights, sounds, smells, temperature, the wind on your face, and the rays of the Sun.

When you feel intuitively that the proper moment has arrived, sit down in a comfortable place. After taking several easy, deep breaths, look around you. Observe the rocks, trees, grasses, flowers, sky. Close your eyes, and continue to breathe deeply for several minutes. Holding the beauty of your surroundings in your mind's eye, feel yourself part of the world around you.

Slowly chant the name Gaia, the Greek Earth goddess, over and over. Feel your love and reverence for her, the mother who loves you, supports you and sustains you. Know that you are one of her beloved children. Enjoy your state of connectedness while you continue to chant for several minutes.

Cease chanting, and in silence, be open to any ideas or impressions that might enter your consciousness. After several minutes, open your eyes and see the natural world around you. Take several deep breaths, and offer Gaia your thanks. Stand slowly and stretch.

Chapter Seven:
Everyday Meditations

Thought Meditation

One of the primary purposes of meditation is to make us more aware of our thought processes. The following meditation is designed to assist in this process of self-awareness.

1. Do one of the Basic Relaxation Exercises. As you breathe, be aware of each thought as it comes up, without censuring it, resisting it, or judging it in any way. Try to observe the connection (if any) of one thought to another.

Watch each thought as it departs, and be aware of the next thought that comes up. Continue this process of active observation for three to five minutes.

3. You will probably find a combination of present-day concerns, old memories, odd associations, and projections for the future. Record your thoughts in a notebook, describing them as you saw them. Write down everything you can remember.

4. If you continue this meditation for several days or weeks, review your notes from time to time, comparing the thoughts that come up each day during your practice.

Empty Space Meditation

In the previous meditation exercise, you observed your thoughts as they came up. The following meditation is similar, yet it helps us focus on the concept of empty space that exists between thoughts.

1. Do one of the Basic Relaxation Exercises. Be aware of each thought as it comes up, without censoring it, resisting it, or judging it in any way. Try to observe the connection (if any) of one thought to another. Watch each thought as it departs, and be aware of the next thought that comes up.

2. Be aware of any space between thoughts: moments of quiet, calm, or emptiness that may be found between your thoughts. Be aware of them without trying to shorten or lengthen them in any way. With practice, these moments of "sacred space" will enlarge.

Meditation for Mind Expansion

1. Sit in a quiet place. Devote several minutes to one of the Basic Relaxation Exercises. When you feel sufficiently relaxed and centered, read a spiritual or other thought-provoking statement. Some possible statements include:

> Let the kingdom of your heart be so wide that no one is excluded. —N. Sri Ram

> He who does not attempt to make peace when small discords arise, is like a bee's hive which leaks drops of honey. Soon, the whole hive collapses. —Nagarjuna

> People ought not to consider so much what they are to do as what they are; let them be good and their ways and deeds will shine brightly. —Meister Eckhart

> The key to humanity's trouble . . . has been to take and not give, to accept and not share, to grasp and not distribute. —Alice A. Bailey

It is in the heart center that our inner nature grows to fullness. Once the heart center opens, all blockages dissolve, and a spirit of intuition spreads throughout our entire body so that our whole being comes alive.

—Tarthang Tulku

2. Devote several minutes to thinking about the idea and exploring its meanings.

3. At the same time, open yourself to inspiration and understanding regarding this idea. At this point, your mind is more alive and expansive, opening itself to new possibilities and ways of perception.

4. Close your eyes and continue to observe your thoughts, being aware of any wandering or unrelated thinking. Gently bring your consciousness back to the concept at hand.

5. After a few minutes, take several deep breaths and conclude your meditation.

Candle Meditation

Fire is one of the primary forces of the universe, and has long been worshiped as a medium of prophecy and as a means of inspiration. Meditating on a burning a candle can help you connect with the spirit within. Not only is a candle aesthetically pleasing, but it can be a source of comfort, especially if you are feeling lonely, upset, or depressed.

1. Sit in a comfortable position, either in a straight-backed chair or on a cushion on the floor. Place a new white candle in front of you and light it.

2. Perform one of the Basic Relaxation Exercises, and pay special attention to your breathing.

3. As you breathe, observe the lighted candle as a symbol of hope and life.

4. If your thoughts wander, try not to follow their trail. Gently bring your mind back to the flame.

5. After ten or so minutes, conclude your meditation and extinguish the candle.

Word Symbol Meditation

Words have power and contain the ability to teach, inspire, harm, or heal. This meditation is designed to help us more deeply understand the power of certain words and feel their creative power.

After performing one of the Basic Relaxation Exercises described earlier, select an index card on which you have clearly written a word in blue or violet ink. As you watch your breathing, place the card before you and spend several minutes pondering the word. Ask yourself the following questions: What does this word mean to me? What associations (if any) does it bring up? How does the word affect me emotionally, mentally, or spiritually?

Continue to be aware of your breathing, and slowly come

out of your meditation. Devote several more minutes to recording your impressions in a journal. You may wish to meditate on a different word each day, or devote several meditations to one specific word of your choice. Some suggested words on which to meditate include:

* Beauty
* Compassion
* Courage
* Creativity
* Detachment
* Discrimination
* Eternal
* God
* Gratitude
* Guru (or Teacher)
* Harmony
* Healing
* Holy
* Hope
* Humility
* Inclusiveness
* Integration
* Light
* Love
* Movement
* Patience
* Peace
* Relinquishing
* Responsibility
* Right Action
* Right Speech
* Right Thought
* Spontaneity
* Surrender
* Trust
* Trustworthiness
* Truthfulness
* Universal
* Wholeness
* Wisdom

Meditating on Numbers

Although primarily used as symbols of quantity, mystics and alchemists in anccient times taught that numbers hold deeper, more subtle meanings, symbolizing universal truths and specific aspects of creation.

Those who practiice the science of numerology believe that each number reflects certain aptitudes and character tendencies. Each letter of your name is given a numerical value, and the sum of the numbers of your name and birth date are believed to offer important insights about your character, life task, talents, and abilities.

The following list contains some of the keynote qualities of the numbers. You may relate other meanings to these numbers through personal experience, and may discover more through meditation. Curiously, a number may reflect a paradox, and contain two completely opposite meanings. For example, the number 0 symbolizes both infinitely large and infinitely small!

0 ✳ **Infinity** universality, totality; the cycles of life; the point at the center; the outer circumference, limitation

1 ✳ **Manifestation** positive or active principle in nature; initiating action, pioneering, leading, selfhood, independence, rulership; God, primary; the fundamental unity of all things; symbol of the Sun

2 ✳ **Antithesis** polarities (positive/negative, male/female,

yin/yang), dualism (spirit and matter, implicit and explicit); unites opposite principles, cooperation, adaptability, mediating, combination, partnering; symbol of the Moon

3 ∗ **Trinity** (Father, Son, Holy Spirit; life, substance, intelligence; father, mother, child; force, matter, consciousness; past, present, future), extension of the self, expression, verbalization, socialization; symbol of Mars

4 ∗ **The material universe** physical laws, logic and reason, cube or square, the intellect distinguishing between the material and spiritual; foundation, order, struggle against limits, slow yet steady growth; symbol of Mercury

5 ∗ **Expansion** increase, fertility, reaping, harvest, material reproduction of self, constructive use of freedom, understanding, judgment; symbol of Jupiter

6 ∗ **Cooperation** uniting, marriage, harmony, peace, resolution, reciprocal action, interaction between spiritual and material, alchemy; symbol of Venus

7 ∗ **Completion** seven days of the week, seven basic colors, seven human temperaments, cycle of evolution, time and space, analysis, understanding, knowledge, awareness; symbol of Saturn

8 ∗ **Dissolution** laws of cyclic evolution, reaction, rupture, disintegration, separation, the incoming breath, genius, inventiveness, high material goals; symbol of Uranus

9 ∗ **Regeneration** travel, going forth, reaching out, giving, selflessness, extension, spirituality, extrasensory perception, new birth, creative expression; symbol of Neptune

The Method

1. Write down each number clearly on an index card to observe while you meditate. You also may want a pen and notebook for this meditation as well.

2. Sit in a comfortable position, either in a straight-baked chair or on a mat or cushion on the floor. Perform one of the Basic Relaxation Exercises.

3. Choose a number on which to meditate. With the different keywords of the number (listed above) in mind, ponder their meaning. What additional meanings does the number hold for you? How do you feel about the number? What significance does it have in your life? Allow your thoughts and feelings to come to the surface, and record them in your journal.

4. After ten minutes, slowly conclude your meditation exercise.

Meditating to Music

Music is a powerful form of energy that can help us enter new and different states of consciousness. On the physical level, music has been shown to cause changes in breathing, muscular tension, heartbeat, and blood pressure. Many of us have found that music can affect us emotionally; it can sooth, inspire, or make us sad or depressed. Harmonious music in particular can create vibratory patterns in our consciousness, and perhaps help us achieve greater harmony in ourselves.

Some types of music can increase the brain's alpha wave activity, often associated with meditative practice. This is one reason why music is frequently used as a prelude to meditation practice, although music itself can become the vehicle or the object of a meditation, whether at home or at a concert.

You may also utilize music while you chant. Music from India and China is especially conducive to mantra meditation. Some recorded chants have accompanying music, so you can simply join in.

1. Before beginning this meditation, choose and play a piece of classical, new age, Indian sitar, or another type of quiet, restful music as you perform one of the Basic Relaxation Exercises.

2. When you are relaxed, listen to the music without interruption for three or more minutes, paying attention to your breathing. Be aware of individual and collective sounds and their relationship to each other. Take note of the harmony, the movement, the entrance and exit of the various instruments. Be aware, too, of how the music makes you feel.

3. It is easy to become lost in daydreams. If you find your mind wandering to unrelated thoughts, gently return your focus to the music itself. At first, devote three or four minutes to this meditation exercise and gradually increase your practice to fifteen minutes or more.

Eating Meditation

As many gourmets can attest, eating can be a spiritual experience. Yet many of us eat primarily to survive, and are often unaware of our food when we eat it. The following meditation is designed to help us feel a deeper connection with the food that nourishes and sustains us.

1. Sit quietly with your food before you. Ideally, confine your meditation to a single type of natural food at first, like an apple, an olive, a carrot, or a few nuts in the shell.

2. Note the color, texture, and aroma of the food. If possible, hold it in your hand and offer thanks to the Great Spirit for the food that you are about to take into your body. Express gratitude to the life form that you are about to eat.

3. In your mind's eye, trace the origins of the food. If you are about to eat an olive, for example, picture the olive tree rooted deep in the earth. Imagine its natural surroundings, including the Sun, rain, and wind. Imagine the olive being picked at its moment of ripeness, and give thanks to the harvester as well as those who prepared the olive and brought it to you today. Devote several minutes to this exercise.

4. Take a small bite of the food. Allow your mouth to experience it fully: the taste, the juice, the texture. Allow your taste buds to enjoy it while appreciating the entirety of your experience. Chew the food slowly and thoroughly.

When the time is right, slowly swallow the food, acknowledging that it is becoming part of your body. Feel your connection to the food, and also feel gratitude for the nourishment; at the same time, feel your connectedness with the source of the food, such as the olive tree or apple tree. Continue to experience the food in this manner until it is completely eaten.

5. Give thanks to the Great Spirit and to the life of the food that you have eaten. Pray that its sacrifice will enable you to be of service to others.

6. Throughout this meditation, be aware of your desire to rush this process and be conscious of any feelings that come up. Do I feel uneasy or guilty about eating? How do I feel when I take another life to sustain my own? How do I disassociate myself from what I eat? Do I eat quietly, or do I pack it in before moving on to another activity? How do I abuse my relationship with food?

With regular practice, this meditation can be expanded to include different foods that are made up of more than one ingredient, such as bread, soup, or tea. If practiced regularly, every single meal can evolve into a meditation that will help expand and deepen your awareness of the life forms that nourish and sustain you. Eating food meditatively will improve digestion and increase overall enjoyment. At the same time, you will eat only what you really need rather than consume excessive amounts.

Meditation for Drivers

During a talk in San Diego some years ago, the Indian teacher J. Krishnamurti turned his focus to meditation. With enthusiasm, he extolled the virtues of meditation, and mentioned that one could meditate anywhere: at home, at school, on a bus . . . even while driving a car . . . quickly adding with a laugh, "but be awfully careful."

With modern distractions like cell phones and an increasing lack of courtesy on the nation's highways, driving (especially in heavy traffic and on the freeways) has become a challenge for many of us. Yet for those who drive, it is important to know that meditation does not imply spacing out behind the wheel. Because the goal of meditation is focused awareness, it can actually increase our potential for safety. In addition to helping make the journey more enjoyable, meditation can help reduce stress and enable us to become both more forgiving and more considerate of others when we are behind the wheel. The following meditation is best done while alone.

1. After you settle into your seat, take several deep breaths, noting any areas of tension in your body. Breathe into those areas of tension, allowing your breathing to dissolve the stress.

2. Pray, "I ask for protection on my journey today, and may I be attentive behind the wheel."

3. Keep your radio and cell phone off as you drive.

Be aware of how you are driving, taking special note of speed, anger, impatience, and daydreaming. If you catch yourself daydreaming, gently move your attention back to your speed, the road, and the other drivers around you. Try to anticipate their moves. Send good feelings to other drivers, including those who would ordinarily make you angry or critical.

Whenever you reach a stop sign or stoplight, take several gentle breaths and review how you are feeling. If you feel tense or anxious, take several deep breaths, and exhale, making a sound like "aaahh."

4. When you arrive at your destination, take a moment to give thanks for a safe trip. Turn off the ignition and mindfully leave your car.

Airplane Meditation

Meditating on an airplane offers unique opportunities. Flying high above the Earth offers a unique perspective of the planet, including the geography, weather patterns, air currents, and the state of the environment over which we pass.

The time you spend on an air journey (especially when traveling alone) can be a form of suspended animation, in which you are disengaged from your daily life responsibilities as well as the people you normally spend time with. Psychically, the stratosphere is a place of rarified energy that facilitates spiritual activities like prayer, meditation, and visualization. The following meditations are designed to help you take advantage of this special airborne environment and to become aware of new perspectives regarding personal perceptions, problems, and aspirations.

I

Sitting comfortably in your seat, close your eyes and breathe deeply yet quietly. Visualize yourself as you are at the moment, moving high above the Earth in total safety, feeling as though you are in the hands of God. Be aware of turbulence or other movements of the aircraft, knowing that you are safe and moving forward on your journey through the vast, unlimited, open sky.

See yourself as free from earthly obligations, including your job, your family, and your daily obligations. You are almost in a state of benign suspension, of emptiness. You are part of life, yet at the same time, detached from it.

II

Close your eyes and remain aware of your breathing. Allow yourself to bring up a thought or a problem that concerns you. View it from your present state of detached awareness. As you breathe comfortably, ask how you might deal with this problem or concern from this detached perspective. Ask: Can I view this issue from my unique perspective of detachment at this time? What can I say or do to improve the situation? How can I move the situation toward a new level of resolution?

Continue to breathe and open your eyes. You are in the world, yet moving high above the Earth. It is truly a special experience. Conclude your meditation and record your impressions in a journal.

III

As you breathe evenly, pray to be open to new ideas and new directions. Close your eyes and allow yourself to envision what you would like to see happen in your life. Do you wish to encourage the emergence of a hidden talent or ability? Do you have a project you would like to begin (or finish)? Is there a relationship you wish to pursue (or change the one you are presently involved in)? Is there a career goal toward which you are striving?

As you continue to watch your breathing, allow your mind to quietly explore the issue. How do you relate to it? What is blocking your fulfillment? How can you see it happen? As you play with these thoughts, be open to any new ideas or perspectives that may come into your consciousness. Enjoy the journey and feel gratitude for the opportunity to explore these important issues in your life.

After several minutes, open your eyes and look around the plane. Then record your impressions and insights in a journal.

Meditations for Right Livelihood

Choosing a career is one of the most important decisions a person can make. Ideally, a career should be more than simply earning a living, but also way to learn, to grow, and to utilize our interests, talents, and abilities.

The concept of "Right Livelihood" was first introduced by the Buddha thousands of years ago. Since that time, Right Livelihood has been viewed as a way of life that develops a sense of self-worth, does good for society, and fosters respect for all living beings. According to Danaan Perry and Lila Forest in *The Earthstewards Handbook*, Right Livelihood needs to encompass the following aspects of life:

* Produce something of personal benefit rather than just material benefit to others.

* Provide a fair return which fulfills our personal needs while not encouraging personal greed.

* Give us a sense of being a valued part of the local and larger community.

* Develop a touchstone of deep experience by which to measure other situations in life.

* Provide genuine personal satisfaction and self-fulfillment.

* Increase skill and the development of our talents and faculties.

* Give expression to the values by which we live.

The following meditations are designed to help develop a deeper sense of Right Livelihood in our lives.

For those searching for a career path

1. Sit in a comfortable position on a straight-backed chair or meditation cushion. Do one of the Basic Relaxation Exercises.

2. Begin to ponder on the right career for you. Ask yourself: What are my major interests? What are my strongest talents? What types of activities give me pleasure and fulfillment? What kind(s) of work would I really like to do? How can I integrate my spiritual beliefs into a career path? What concrete steps do I need to take in order to move ahead?

3. Allow your ideas and feelings to come to the surface, without judging them or censoring them in any way. Record them in your journal.

4. Continue this meditation exercise for ten minutes. Take a few deep breaths, stretch, and slowly leave the seated meditation position.

For those already on a career path

1. Sit in a comfortable position on a straight-backed chair or meditation cushion. Do one of the Basic Relaxation Exercises.

2. Begin to ponder on your career, writing your

observations in a journal. Rather than focusing on changing it, think about what originally drew you to it in the first place. Ask yourself questions like: How does it mobilize my talents? Did I originally feel passion towards this work? What are the sources of my dissatisfaction at the present time? Are there ways to deal with them? If so, how? How can I make my career more in line with the teaching about Right Livelihood? Do I need a total change of direction? If so, what do I need to do in order to take the next step?

3. Allow your thoughts and feelings to surface without judging or censoring them in any way. Some may provide vital information to enable you to take the next step in your career direction.

4. Continue this meditation exercise for ten minutes. Take a few deep breaths, stretch, and slowly leave the seated meditation position.

Chapter Eight: Meditations for Deepening the Self

Seeking Wisdom

In traditional cultures, community members often have access to a wise elder who is a source of instruction and advice. The elder, whether shaman or medicine person, is regarded as a type of community treasure, whose advice is highly valued by tribal members. This person helps members access their own innate wisdom by telling stories or asking questions. However, most of us today do not have access to a wise and trusted "elder" who can offer us clarity and vision when we are facing a difficult problem.

The following exercise is designed to help us access wisdom in our life by contacting "the sage within" through meditation.

1. Perform one of the Basic Relaxation Exercises described earlier.

2. Close your eyes. Imagine that you are in the presence of a sage: a wise person of limitless knowledge and compassion. Know also that this person is very concerned about your welfare, and is eager to help you in any way possible. Imagine yourself making respectful contact with this elder.

3. Ask this person a question about an issue that has been troubling you: it may concern a problem in your relationship, an important career decision, or a question about how you can improve your health. Continue to be aware of your breathing as you ask this question.

4. Allow yourself to be receptive to whatever response may come up. You may receive a direct answer, or you may be asked another question in return. Allow yourself to be open to whatever answer you receive.

5. After several minutes, express gratitude to this person and take leave of him or her. Conclude your meditation.

6. Write your experiences in a journal. You may not receive a final answer to your question in one session. It is possible that the information you receive during your meditation may lead to additional questions to ponder before you arrive at a satisfactory solution. With practice, this meditation can become an important learning tool.

Daily Review Meditation

Human beings are made up of a variety of often contradictory currents. We have qualities that we view as positive, like compassion, humor, courage, and openness to new ideas. We also have qualities we call negative, like jealousy, possessiveness, fearfulness, and dishonesty. Very often, we tend to ignore the negative currents, or downplay their significance in our lives.

It is not unlike having to deal with a noisy child who constantly demands our attention: We want him to leave us in peace, so we may either ignore him or send him to his room. Similarly, we often ignore our negative feelings or simply pretend that they do not exist. Unfortunately, like children who feel that they are being ignored by their parents, the negative feelings demand our attention with greater and greater intensity. When unresolved feelings are not dealt with directly, they often create situations in our life that force us to deal with them anyway. Very often these situations form a pattern. Our difficulties, though we often judge them to be "bad," can provide us with the stepping stones to enable us to make positive changes in our ways of thinking and feeling.

Spiritual teachers have told us that one of the goals of meditation is to explore what are known as "lower self issues" in order to transform them into positive qualities. Like digging through a layer of mud and dirt to uncover a buried treasure, so must we dig through the "dirt" of our lower nature to discover our universal soul.

There are many ways to achieve this, including psychotherapy, body-oriented therapies like Core Energetics and bioenergetics, and other self-awareness techniques. Another way is through daily review meditations. As reflected by their names, these meditations are most effective when done on a daily basis.

Evening Daily Review

The best time to do this meditation is when you are ready for bed. You may also wish to do it whenever you are having trouble sleeping due to worry or another form of emotional disturbance. In order to do this meditation, have a notebook or journal at hand, as well as a quiet place where you can be alone.

1. Sit quietly for several minutes at the end of your day. Take several deep, gentle breaths and affirm that you wish to explore areas of your being that have caused you difficulty during the day. You may make a prayer of your own, or simply say, "I pray to explore areas of my being that have caused me difficulty today."

2. After several minutes of receptive silence, write down keywords or sentences describing situations or feelings that caused disharmony in your life during the day. Be completely honest and candid in your statements, which are intended to be only between you and God. "I lost my temper with my wife today," or "I spread gossip about my coworker today," would be two examples.

Such statements may reveal resentment, jealousy, anger, sadness, feelings of low self-esteem, or acts of deception. Though you may feel ashamed about these feelings or actions, write them down anyway. They are all part of you and make up part of your internal "family."

Be careful not to judge yourself or make the feelings or actions worse than they really are. Remember that even the most uncomfortable or shameful situation can be a stepping stone to spiritual fulfillment.

3. Continue to write for seven to ten minutes. Be mindful of how your thoughts, feelings, and actions caused disharmony during the day. When you've finished writing, say, "I ask God (or the Great Spirit) to help me transform areas of disharmony within my being."

4. Over the days and weeks that you will do this meditation, you will notice that clear patterns often reveal themselves. Ask yourself:

- ✳ How do they appear?
- ✳ When do they come up and with whom?
- ✳ How do they cause disharmony in my life?
- ✳ What role do I have in creating this inner disharmony?
- ✳ How can I change these negative currents?

5. Over weeks and months of regular meditation, you will become more aware of the geography of your lower nature. You will also become aware of many of the subtle tricks that you have used to avoid recognizing and dealing with difficult issues. By bringing disharmonious issues to light, you will find that you can work with them more effectively, and transform negative currents into positive qualities that bring inner peace and greater awareness. Continue to ask God (or your higher self) for help with any area in your life that continues to cause you difficulty.

Morning Daily Review

Like the evening daily review, many people who enjoy writing can practice a simple morning meditation that can help them achieve greater harmony and awareness during the day.

1. Sit quietly for a few minutes, taking regular breaths.

2. Ask God or your higher self for help in exploring

areas that are of concern to you as you begin your day.

3. While in a receptive state, simply write down phrases or key words that describe feelings of disharmony or concern. These may have to do with your feeling anger toward another person, anxiety about an interview at work, or fears about money or health. As in the evening daily review, simply write down whatever comes up without making judgments about it. Write for seven to ten minutes.

4. Read what you have written down. Ask God or your higher self to help you be aware of these issues during the day, and ask for help in transforming them and dealing with them from a place of intelligence and higher understanding.

As you explore these issues at the beginning of every day, you can relate to them with greater clarity and purpose. Over time, you will see that this morning meditation will allow you to understand the inner meaning of troublesome issues, and how they can be a catalyst for spiritual growth and inner peace.

Getting to Know Your Potential Self Meditation

Sit in a straight-backed chair. Adjust your body so it is comfortable, with your spine straight, your palms facing up on your thighs, and your feet flat on the floor.

Slowly close your eyes and start to breathe purposefully, deeply, and rhythmically.

Continue to breathe deeply as you count from one to ten. The higher the number, the more deeply relaxed you become.

"One."

"Two."

"Three."

"Four."

Feel the energy pulsate through your body,
as you watch your breath.

"Five."

"Six."

"Seven."

You feel that the boundaries of your body
are gently disappearing.

"Eight."

"Nine."

"Ten."

Your mind is awake while your physical body is at rest.

Now, imagine that your mind has expanded beyond the boundaries of your body. It is free from physical tension and body limitations. You can now experience profound insights and life-transforming breakthroughs.

Using all your senses, including sight, smell, hearing,

touch, and taste, imagine that you are standing in a meadow near a flowing stream. You feel very comfortable here. There are flowers everywhere. An apple orchard is in the background, and the trees are all in full bloom. Birds are singing. Bees and other insects are humming. You can hear the sound of water splashing on the rocks, and you can smell the spring flowers. The sky is blue, the air is crisp, and you feel a slight breeze on your face.

What do you see? What colors are there? What do you smell? What sounds do you hear? What do you feel touching you? What emotions do you feel? Feel the peace that is here.

While you are in this place of peace and beauty, imagine that you see a friendly figure approaching you. As you observe, imagine that the person coming toward you is you—at your fullest potential. What qualities do you have within that are manifested in your life now? What do you look like? What qualities does that person have that you have not yet expressed in your life? Feel the kindness, the strength, and the enthusiasm that this person has as he/she walks toward you.

What is the chosen life path of that individual? What qualities has he/she developed? Breathe gently and continue to observe this person.

Now, imagine that this person has a message to share with you. What is the message? Can you open your ears to hear it? Hear it now.

Finally, imagine this person walking up to you and making eye contact. See the love and understanding in the eyes of your realized self. Acknowledge your connectedness and love for each other.

Now slowly begin counting down from ten to one.

"Ten."

"Nine."

"Eight."

"Seven."

You feel both an inner calm and a deep connection to your true self.

"Six."

"Five."

"Four."

"Three."

"Two."

"One."

You are wide awake and alert, both physically and mentally. You feel rested and relaxed, with an inner calm and a deep connection to your true self. You will retain an inner knowing of who you are as you live your daily life.

Remember that through this meditation, you can return any time you want to enjoy the peace of this place and commune with your full potential self.

The Four Facets of Loving

Understanding the meaning of love is one of life's great challenges. Poets, religious leaders, and philosophers have written volumes about what it means to truly love. Many agree that there are four important factors that allow love to thrive: compassion, understanding, freedom from judgment and listening. In fact, all of these aspects are intimately related, and together lay the groundwork for a positive self-image, successful relationships, and a life of purpose and fulfillment.

Focus on one quality each morning for four mornings, although you may want to repeat the four-day cycle regularly. It is also valuable to record your experiences in a journal. This will be useful when you reflect on your life from time to time, and can also serve as the foundation for personal meditation themes in the future.

Sit in a comfortable posture, either in a straight-backed chair or on a cushion placed on the floor. Do one of the Basic Relaxation Exercises described earlier. Light a white candle if you wish.

Compassion

1. Before you begin, you might pray or affirm: "I wish to explore the meaning of compassion in my life today."

2. Pen and notebook in hand, ponder the elements of compassion. What does the word mean to you? How do people manifest compassion in life? Think of people you know who are in need (including some who may not be easy to deal with). Send them feelings of compassion at this time. How can you share compassion with people, animals, and plants in your daily life? How can you show greater compassion toward yourself?

3. Observe your thoughts and feelings as you explore these issues, without evaluating them or censoring them in any way. Record them in your notebook. After ten minutes, conclude your meditation.

Understanding

1. Before you begin, you might pray or affirm: "I wish to explore the elements of understanding in my life today."

2. Pen and notebook at hand, ask yourself what are the elements of understanding? What facilitates them and what stops them from taking place? Who do I have trouble understanding in my life? For today, agree to place yourself in their situation and take on their point of view. Know that although you do not need to agree with them, the goal today is to deepen your level of understanding.

3. Observe your thoughts and feelings as you explore these issues, without evaluating them or censoring them in any way. Be especially aware of any currents of justification and resistance you may have.

4. Record your impressions in your notebook. After ten minutes, conclude your meditation.

Freedom from Judgment

1. Before you begin, pray or affirm: "I pray to explore my tendency to judge people and situations today."

2. Pen and notebook at hand, devote several minutes to exploring how you judge yourself, other people, and situations in your life. Be specific and record these instances in your journal. Ask yourself: What are the currents behind my judgmental attitude? How do I feel when I judge myself and others? How does judging destroy understanding and compassion? Be aware of your thoughts and feelings as they come up and record them in your journal.

3. Today, commit yourself to being aware of making judgments about yourself, other people, and situations in which you find yourself. Remember that it may be too early to take a vacation from making judgments. Your goal today is to be aware of them and their ramifications in your relationships with others.

4. Conclude your meditation with a few deep breaths and stretches.

Listening

1. Before you begin, pray or affirm: "I pray to understand the importance of listening."

2. Explore your reactions when others speak with you. Do you think about a response before they finish talking to you? Do you hear their words but don't really listen to them? Do you interrupt them? Do you tune out when you hear things that make you uncomfortable or that you don't like? How do you feel when you do this? How do you feel when others don't listen to you? Cite specific instances with specific people. Write them down in your journal.

3. Ponder on the elements that are involved in truly listening to others. Record them in your notebook.

4. Commit yourself to being aware of not listening when you converse with others today. Conclude your meditation with several deep breaths and stretches.

Meditations for Deepening Love and Enhancing Sexual Expression

Psychologists and others who have probed the workings of the human mind have found that the power of the unconscious is much greater than we realize. Because it functions primarily from emotional memory and deep psychological patterns of which we are often unaware, its workings are not readily available for us to clearly see. When we want something to happen or consciously believe in a possibility or an idea, we often find that our experience is different or even opposite our conscious desire. As a result, we may feel disappointed and victimized. This is because our unconscious fears and attitudes have a powerful impact on our outer reality, no matter what our conscious desires may be. For this reason, it is important for us to try to make the unconscious conscious. One of the best ways to achieve this is through meditation and creative visualization.

The following meditations are based on the book Lovelight: Unveiling the Mysteries of Love and Romance, by Julia Bondi and Nathaniel Altman (Pocket Books, 1989). They are most effective when practiced after several minutes of deep breathing and relaxation.

Letting Go

All of us are carrying around fears, anxieties and other emotional baggage from our past. These inevitably project themselves into our relationships. The following meditation is designed to help us free ourselves from these negative images and feelings. It is best to do it in a quiet setting with candlelight.

You are going to take a trip to a special resort, which is located in an area well known for its hot springs and healing waters. Surrounding this mountain retreat is a soothing pine forest. You are going to remain at this retreat as long as you wish for healing and rejuvenation.

Imagine yourself at the resort. You are walking through

the pine forest and see many separate streams that flow into one large and beautiful pool. The air is crisp and clean. It has the scent of freshness. You instinctively know you will be able to heal yourself completely in this sylvan setting.

As you pass the streams, you see a small sign identifying the symptom which the waters will purify. There is a stream for every possible fear, including yours. By bathing in these waters, you will be able to experience a complete release of all the negativity from your present and from your past. Remove your robe and ease yourself into the stream that suits your needs. Remain in the running water until you feel totally cleansed.

When you are ready, proceed to any other stream that will heal the fears you experience. After you have been cleansed by the healing waters, you feel ready to immerse yourself in the pool of self-love. You dive into the fresh, clear water and find that it is just the perfect temperature for you. There are bubbles of effervescence teasing your skin. You immediately begin to relax and feel refreshed. The pool of self-love is the ultimate healing. The waters have washed away all beliefs and attitudes that have caused stress and negativity in the past.

You can perform this meditation whenever you wish. Each time you do it you will feel a deeper level of cleansing. Experiment with the streams to see which ones you require at any particular time. Always finish the exercise with a swim in the pool of self-love into which all the other streams flow.

Experiencing Sexuality

Getting in touch with our sexual feelings is natural, appropriate, and expansive. It is vital for our health and well-being at physical, emotional, mental, and spiritual levels.

I Flame Energy Visualize or feel a flame of red energy in the root chakra that burns brightly in the sexual organs, suffusing them with warmth. Expand this sexual fire in an upward spiral toward the higher chakras. Move the flame upward, one chakra at a time, until the spiral of fire (often experienced as sensual heat) suffuses and warms your entire body.

II Serpentine Spiral See or feel a serpent coiled at the base of your spine. Vocalize either the chant "Hum," so that it vibrates through your body or the "Om-ta-ma-ra-om" that balances all the body's energies. As you make these sounds, see the serpent gradually rise in a spiral up through the chakras, one by one, until the serpent's head reaches the crown chakra while the serpent's tail is located in the root chakra, its body coiled throughout the intermediate chakras. Feel the power and undulating movement of the serpent.

The image of the coiled snake rising in an unfolding spiral was used extensively in ancient cultures (especially in Egypt) as a symbol of the creative unfolding spiral of life energy. Because the snake sheds its skin and emerges reborn, snakes were seen as symbols of transformation.

III Energy Reservoir See or feel the universe as a pool or reservoir of unlimited primal sexual energy out of which all creation has come. Feel yourself linked to that reservoir with a silver cord (like an umbilical cord) entering the body at the root chakra. Imagine that, with the aid of a pump that is at hand, you can utilize as much of that energy as you want and need at any time. There is a switch on the pump that you can turn on or off at will. Feel the energy pumped up through each chakra, filling it with warm, vibrant light and pulsating energy. This enlivens you.

IV Finding the Purpose of the Relationship Each partner in a relationship can take a journey into the world of imagery through creative meditation. At first, take the journey alone. After several journeys, you might invite your partner to join you. To make sure you feel comfortable with your partner participating in the journey, first try this as a visualization. Later you can sit together and take the journey in person. Answers will begin to appear, revealing more as your relationship grows and deepens.

After doing one of the Basic Relaxation Exercises, begin at the entrance to a large forest where there are a variety of trails. Each trail is marked with a sign labeled: "Soul Purpose," "Past-Life Connection," "Present Opportunity," "Solution to Existing Problems," or other words of your choosing. Each time you do this meditation, you can choose the path on which you most desire to tread. Once on your chosen path, you will notice that there are arrows or signs before every curve along the way; these signs not only indicate the direction, but offer clues, hints, or other pieces of information that help deal with your question.

At the end of the path is a clearing, where you discover a beautiful shrine, temple, or church. Steps lead up to the entrance of this holy place, where a guide awaits with the knowledge and wisdom you need about the path you have chosen.

V Finding Your Soul Mate Most of us desire to find a partner with whom we can share our lives totally, yet we don't know how to go about finding him or her. The following meditation and imagery technique will prepare you for the experience of finding your soul mate.

After performing one of the Basic Relaxation Exercise, imagine yourself going into a complex that houses a powerful computer. The computer contains all the information available in the world. Its database is universal and contains a complete dossier on every person alive.

As you enter, a person comes to greet you. You are treated as a special guest. Your host explains the incredible capacity of this computer, and you are told that it is entirely at your disposal. You are asked to be seated and are offered a special request form for the ideal mate. The staff is available during this process to provide whatever assistance you require.

Visualize yourself listing all of the qualities that you desire in a mate, such as sensitivity, sexual attractiveness, intelligence, or a sense of humor. Once you complete the form, a staff member submits this data to the computer for you, and your host returns to assure you that nothing more need be done, since the computer will search all its data until it locates your ideal mate.

With complete confidence in the process, you return home to await notification. A short time later, you receive a notice confirming that your request has been filled. Your soul mate is ready to meet you and will arrive with no further effort on your part.

By doing this meditation, you establish the expectation that there is an ideal mate for you, and that the universe is busy finding your mate and bringing that person to you.

Chapter Nine: Meditation with Runes

A Brief History

According to the early Norse peoples, as our universe began, so did the runes. Runes told the story of the origins of the cosmos, and also provided a way to pass this information from one generation to the next. As they epresent all the cosmic energies, they form a kind of ancient treasure map, leading to divinity.

Runic letter rows begin with the letters F, U, TH, A, R, K, and because of this are named Futharks. The most ancient of these is the Elder Futhark, with its twenty-four runes, which is the one we work with here. It is divided into three groups of eight, called the aettir. In Old Norse, the words aett (singular) and aettir (plural) mean generation(s) and/or family(ies). The word aett also linguistically relates to the number eight.

Some recent theories about the origins of the runes are:

1) The Elder Futhark is of the same origin as the ancient Turkish inscriptions of the Gokturk alphabet.

2) Runes appeared in Scandinavia between 1800 and 400 B.C.E. There is evidence that the Goths learned the art of runes before they left Scandinavia, between 200 B.C.E. and 200 C.E.

3) Norwegian runes are identical to runes used in Semitic-language areas, such as Trojan Asia Minor and Canaan (Palestine) as far back as 2000 B.C.E. New archeological finds show that people from the Mediterranean area, especially Semitic people from Crete, often traveled north on trading tours.

The First Aett

FEHU (fay-hoo)

Element: Fire
Color: Red
Numerological Value: 1
Astrology: Aries
Tarot Card: The Magician
Tree: Elder

Gemstones: Ruby, garnet, red cat's-eye, rose quartz, blood agate, carnelian, jasper

Key Words: Prosperity, mobile wealth, abundance, fertility, unstructured creativity, the primal fire

Mythology: Fehu is the raw archetypal energy of motion and expansion in Oneness which acted as the source of the cosmic fire that produced our human world. This fire represents not only creation but also destruction, reflecting the energetic polarities inherent in all things.

Magical Qualities:

* Strengthens intuitive abilities
* Serves as channel for transferring, projecting, and sending runic energy
* Draws the celestial energies of the Sun, Moon, and stars into your personal energy field
* Increases monetary wealth
* Increases your wealth of knowledge
* Increases the fertility of your life goals and plans

Meaning in Divination: A mobile form of power; embodies the directed, expansive power that moves energy outward from people and objects; manifests in healing energy, primal expansive motion, and prayers or blessings.

The two lines extending upward look like the horns of a cow; also like a person with hands raised and outstretched-

traditionally a pose used by priests and priestesses for prayers and blessings. Fehu symbolizes communing with the gods and goddesses, where a person's field of intention moves into the many dimensions of Oneness. As mobile wealth, this rune also represents money and the things it can buy.

Fehu is unbridled creative fire that has no boundaries, no real structure or form, intimidating to some people because it seems uncontrollable. But if you merge and become one with it, a great burst of creative fire results, to create and fuel your personal meditation patterns. With Fehu, be careful not to burn yourself out, but feel the energy in every cell, until you become energized physically, mentally, and spiritually.

URUZ (ooo-ruse)

Element: Water
Color: Dark green
Numerological Value: 2
Astrology: Taurus
Tarot Card: Strength
Tree: Birch
Gemstones: Emerald, green agate, malachite, aventurine, green beryl, chrysoprase, jade, green tourmaline
Key Words: Patterning force, structure, formation, wisdom, inner strength
Mythology: As Fehu provides creative fire, Uruz provides the structure for this creativity. Together they form the basic

forces that created the world, continue to sustain it, and will eventually destroy it. In a real sense, this sequence of birth, life, and death plays itself out not only on a lifetime level, but in every day of our lives. Every time we get up in the morning, move through the day, and then go to sleep at night, we are essentially acting out this basic sequence. In an esoteric or shamanic sense, this sequence brings transition, growth, and knowledge.

Magical Qualities:

  * Draws energies together to create a magical pattern
  * Heals both physical and mental ailments
  * Promote knowledge and understanding of the self
  * Possess magical strength and power
  * Increases business opportunities
  * Accesses the lays of power or streams of energy within the Earth
  * Brings energy together and helps you realize your goals.

Meaning in Divination: Uruz embodies the cosmic order; growth that is gained by overcoming obstacles; the force that moves you to assert yourself in the world. Uruz is the primal power and stands for seeking new life goals and increasing the energy present in old ones. This rune helps to stabilize and balance, heal illnesses, and settle disputes.

It's important not to be too rigid as you structure your

goals, but to remain flexible enough to adapt to situations and your surroundings. Uruz provides an excellent vehicle for getting in touch with your strengths and weaknesses. By examining the energetic patterns that take place every second of the day, you can learn to influence this energy to your benefit. Everything is energy, and energy has pattern, and pattern has structure. The Uruz rune embodies the concept of pattern, and thus in a very basic sense has to do with the way Oneness is structured.

THURISAZ (thur–ee–saws)

Element: Fire
Color: Red
Numerological Value: 3
Astrology: Mars
Tarot Card: Justice
Tree: Oak
Gemstones: Bloodstone, garnet, red jasper, obsidian, onyx, black tourmaline
Key Words: Protection, destruction, defense, polarity, action, regeneration
Mythology: Thurisaz is a symbol of lightning and thunder, equated with the hammer of Thor. Thor was related to the giants-called "thursars." Thursars are the enormous, ancient, and wise creatures who fought against the gods. They represent the primal elemental forces in nature.

Magical Qualities:

* Actively protects from enemies and harm
* Overcomes unfriendly situations
* Produces love magic
* Awakens your will and helps you take action
* Promotes awareness of the separation and commonality of all things
* Projects energy and applied power

Meaning in Divination: Thurisaz embodies the life-death polarity, either active energy directed outward or passive energy contained and directed inward. It acts mostly as a carrier, and combines well with various other runes to ensure success when you're doing works of meditation. Thurisaz is also associated with the forces of fertilization and regeneration. It breaks down barriers and sets the stage for new beginnings. This rune warns not rush headlong into things but think them through first.

The first two runes, Fehu and Uruz, embody an unconscious or unmanifested dynamic force. As Thurisaz enters the aett, this runic force moves to the edge of consciousness. Its energy is neither totally unconscious, as with the first two runes, nor totally conscious, as with the following rune, Ansuz, which governs consciousness. Thurisaz remains on the edge, between the unmanifested and the manifested, slightly submerged. It resides in the levels of the unconscious mind that are easily accessible. A negative side of this rune appears in the shadows of the unconscious mind, the repressed aspects of your being that, when not dealt with, can fester and become potentially dangerous.

ANSUZ (awn-sooz)

Element: Air
Color: Dark blue
Numerological Value: 4
Astrology: Pluto
Tarot Card: Death
Tree: Ash
Gemstones: Sodalite, aquamarine, sapphire, lapis lazuli, labradorite, jade
Key Words: Order, rebirth, consciousness, knowledge, wisdom, mental agility, communication, creative expression, reason
Mythology: While the giants and the Thurisaz rune symbolize chaos, Ansuz symbolizes order and the Aesir-the gods who descended from Odin. Ansuz is Odin's rune, reflecting his role as the numinous god of magic and ecstasy-the poetic mead of inspiration and the vessel that contained it are concepts closely associated with Odin and Ansuz.

Magical Qualities:

* Increases magical powers and intuitive abilities
* Gets in touch with divine power and knowledge
* Communicates with the divine within
* Inspires the creative arts (speech, song, and writing)
* Assists in times of transformation
* Shape-shifts and works with power animals

Meaning in Divination: On a practical level, Ansuz is the counter-balance to Thurisaz. The divine order that stays firm, no matter how difficult conditions become, stands as a counter-balance to the chaos inherent in the universe. As Thurisaz is used to fetter and protect, Ansuz is used to unfetter and release. The Ansuz rune can be used for releasing the chains that bind us. This is also true for psychological fetters, such as anxieties, fears, and phobias.

Ansuz is the receiver and container, as well as the trans-former and expression of spiritual power and divine knowl-edge. Humankind expresses it through acts of a divine, reli-gious, or magical nature.

With the energy inherent in Ansuz, you can begin to give definite form to your goals and aspirations. Use Thurisaz to protect your spiritual works and patterns, and Ansuz to set the stage for bringing them to life. By merging with Ansuz, you touch divine energy both within and without.

RAIDHO *(rye-tho)*

Element: Air
Color: Red
Numerological Value: 5
Astrology: Sagittarius
Tarot Card: The Chariot
Tree: Oak
Gemstones: Carnelian, rutilated quartz, golden topaz, ruby, purple-red amethyst, aventurine, sugilite
Key Words: Circular flow, rhythm, movement, travel, progression, riding, journey
Mythology: Raidho represents the forces that move the energies of Oneness in a circle. This circular flow is embedded in both the daily and annual solar wheel. Raidho is the rune of divination and ritual or magical ceremony. It helps divine energy to flow from one place to another.

The journey of the Sun in its annual course from north to south and back again, was seen as the procession of the gods of fertility, Nerthus (Earth Mother) and Frey. Such cosmic transportation is denoted by Raidho, demonstrating primal forces controlled by conscious thought.

Magical Qualities:

* Use in ritual, particularly with the Great Days and Full Moons
* Moves runic energy toward a specific destination
* Increases your connection to the cyclic flow of life

* Uses sunwise movement for personal empowerment in magic
* Works with the runic streams of energy
* Connects with the transforming powers of the god(dess)
* Expands your conscious thought processes

Meaning in Divination: Raidho deals with the cycles of existence and how each leads to another. Reaching the goal is not an end, but a transformation and new beginning. This rune embodies the intentional channeling of runic energies and natural laws along the road that leads to the best result. Rhythm and dance also are important to Raidho.

Raidho is the wagon rune, containing the elements of Earth, Water (ice), Air, and Fire, as well as the different states of matter: solid, fluid, gaseous, and transforming.

The negative polarity of Raidho manifests as going around in circles and not getting anywhere. Remember that each cycle (circle) is part of a larger cycle. By keeping the larger picture in perspective, you lessen your chances of moving aimlessly in circles.

KENAZ (kane-awz)

Element: Fire
Color: Gold
Numerological Value: 6
Astrology: Venus
Tarot Card: The High Priestess

Key Words: The rune of knowledge, the internal or controlled fire, guiding light

Tree: Pine

Gemstones: Citrine, fire opal, carnelian, golden topaz, amber, beryl

Mythology: From Kenaz comes fire, the fire of spirit as well as the fire that lights the darkness. It was fire coming into contact with ice that created steam and water, providing the perfect fertile environment for the creation and development of life. Kenaz in particular refers to human fire, and because of this it is called the "human rune," or rune of humankind.

Magical Qualities:

* Inspires creativity
* Strengthens your abilities in all realms
* Regenerates and heals
* Helps in personal transformation
* Manifests through polarities
* Used in love and sexual relationships
* Increases fertility
* Increases personal insight

Meaning in Divination: Kenaz is the rune of human passion, lust, and sexual love as positive attributes through the working of polarities, including that of male and female. From these polarities comes a union that results in manifestation.

Kenaz brings about change and transformation, making it the emotional root of creativity. This change becomes accessible through the controlled power of the psyche, combined with the contained energy of nature, in the achievement of a tangible objective.

The rune is also important in relationships with kin, especially a bonding of the energy of the living and dead members of the family. This bonding creates an energetic link that moves beyond earthly existence. In addition, the concept of kin can be expanded to include a wider grouping, such as like-minded people of similar origins.

Kenaz is the fire that brings life to your goals and aspirations, the point at which your creations begin to take on a life of their own. When you pull this rune, it is time to nurture your spiritual patterns, all the while building up the life force, so that, like children, the patterns can thrive on their own.

GEBO (gay-bow)

Element: Air
Color: Deep blue
Numerological Value: 7
Astrology: Pisces
Tarot Card: Lovers
Tree: Ash/Elm
Gemstones: Sapphire, aquamarine, fluorite, azurite, lapis

lazuli, sodalite, rose quartz, amethyst, jade, kunzite

Key Words: Connection, gift, exchange, interaction, balance

Mythology: Gebo is the rune of deity, that magical power present in the energetically charged void that was in place before the formation of the worlds. Gebo represents the gifts given to humans by the gods and also embodies the gifts that humans give to the gods in return for the gift of life. There is no part of us that is not of Divine origin. In turn, there is no part of the Divine that is not part of us. Gebo, signifies this relationship that flows both ways.

Magical Qualities:

* Initiates magic
* Inspires love magic
* Encourages sacred sexual expression
* Embodies mystical union of the goddess and god
* Increases harmony in relationships
* Reconciles polarities
* Harmoniously connects runic streams of energy
* Accesses Divine Wisdom

Meaning in Divination: On the highest level, the gift transcends both giver and receiver. When including the Gebo rune in sending energies toward a goal, remember that the law of compensation dictates that any displacement or movement of energy has to be compensated in some way. With Gebo, the movement is a gift that moves from giver to receiver and sets up a chain of energetic patterns that culminates in a balancing.

One aspect of Gebo involves the sacred mystery of two (or many) into One. The power of Gebo binds people together to create a specific result. An example of this is sacred sexual expression-the exchange of energetic polarities that produces an intended and desired result. When doing meditation work, you can also use Gebo to bind two or more runes together. Energetically, Gebo represents the reconciliation and merging of opposing energies, such as male and female.

WUNJO (woon-yo)

Element: Earth
Color: Gold
Numerological Value: 8
Astrology: Leo
Tarot Card: The Sun
Tree: Ash
Gemstones: Diamond, golden topaz, amber, citrine, rutilated quartz, clear quartz, herkimer diamond
Key Words: Joy, pleasure, hope, delight, kinship, fellowship, wonderment
Mythology: From Wunjo come acts of magic and the realization of true will.

Magical Qualities:
  ∗ Strengthens social links and bonds
  ∗ Increases your sense of joy and happiness
  ∗ Binds runes towards specific purposes
  ∗ Accesses your ancestral family ties, which can
  be on many energy levels
  ∗ Links runic energies together into one

Meaning in Divination: The depiction is akin to the weather vane on an old barn, showing which way the wind blows. Because of its ability to "turn things around"-to change situations to your advantage-Wunjo is the ideal rune to turn the tide and ensure victory.

Wunjo stands for the mystery of the harmonious existence of varied, but complementary energies. It binds different energetic fields together, and is therefore an invaluable rune in meditation. Also, because it is connected to wishes, it is one of the most energetically charged runes. In the Thurisaz rune, this power is no more than a potentiality, while in Wunjo it becomes fully realized. When used correctly, Wunjo puts you in touch with great power, and helps you actualize your goals and aspirations.

Wunjo brings good fortune, joy, and rewards, and is therefore is perceived as the happiness rune. It also symbolizes Oneness, including both the Divine and material worlds.

The Second Aett

HAGALAZ (haw-ga-laws)

Element: Water

Color: Gray or white

Numerological Value: 9

Astrology: Aquarius

Tarot Card: The World

Tree: Yew/Ash

Gemstones: Clear quartz, diamond, moonstone, opal, clear calcite, geode

Key Words: Transformation, change, evolution, merging, harmony, protection, the past

Mythology: The creation myth describes the Norns, three giant maidens. They are the most powerful of all deities—not even the Aesir could undo what they had done. The Norn maiden of the past, named Urd, rules over the Hagalaz rune.

Magical Qualities:

* Connects runic energies into one
* Assists in personal change and transformation
* Assesses ancestral memory
* Protects from harm
* Promotes shamanic journeying
* Shape-shifts
* Heals past physical, mental, and spiritual wounds

* Increases mystical experiences and knowledge

Meaning in Divination: Hagalaz is the rune of friendship, stability, and bonding. It reveals that from primal chaos, normally thought a destructive force, comes the potential for positive transformation. Every energetic death carries the potential for rebirth and positive personal growth.

Hagalaz often relates to conflicting or disruptive forces originating in the unconscious, creating the potential for change. It is also the rune of self-sabotage due to behavioral patterns that came from the past (Urd). Both Urd and Hagalaz are associated with the realm of the individual unconscious, and with the collective unconscious. This rune has the capacity for extreme polarities-the ultimate good or complete destruction.

hematite
smoky quartz

NAUDHIZ (now-these)

Element: Fire

Color: Black

Numerological Value: 10

Astrology: Capricorn

Tarot Card: The Fool

Tree: Beech

Gemstones: Hematite, obsidian, onyx, smoky quartz

Key Words: Need, help, resistance, deliverance from distress, love, passion, shadow self

Mythology: Naudhiz represents the breath of life and manifestation. Naudhiz is closely associated with the youngest Norn of the three, named Skuld, who rules the future. Skuld's face was always veiled, symbolizing the unseen aspect of the future.

Magical Qualities:
  * Protects
  * Helps you make better choices
  * Assists with divination
  * Increases powers of clairvoyance
  * Meets and works with your spirit guides and power animals
  * Understands your needs and desires
  * Fuels your magical patterns
  * Overcomes psychological obstacles such as bad habits

Meaning in Divination: Naudhiz represents the concept of necessity, layered with the friction that leads to transformation. Strongly associated with love and the heat of passion, friction produces heat, which in turn produces fire. When used with knowledge and wisdom, the need-fire becomes creative and procreative, but when used unwisely this energy becomes a force for destruction that burns like wildfire, leaving only ashes.

Embodying resistance, Naudhiz is a cumulative synthesis, a product of a thesis and antithesis: distress coupled with the guidance to deal with it and move beyond the problem.

Because Naudhiz contains sexual elements, it is a powerful rune to meditate upon to deepen feelings of love. It is also an excellent choice to enhance feelings of protection, especially spiritual protection.

ISA (ee-saw)

Element: Water
Color: White
Numerological Value: 11
Astrology: The waning, crescent Moon
Tarot Card: The Hermit
Tree: Alder
Gemstones: Milky quartz, clear quartz, opal, moonstone
Key Words: Stasis, constraint, slow expansion, massive force, gradual integration, delay
Mythology: Isa embodies primal ice, as well as a stillness and lack of vibration, concepts as primal as that of "spirit." Ice and Fire are the forces that created the world and, in turn, they are the energies that will ultimately destroy it. The giant Norn named Verdandi, who presides over the present, rules the Isa rune.

Magical Qualities:
  * Works with concentration and intention
  * Looks at the form of patterns
  * Slows down energy without stopping it

- Balances and integrates your ego
- Understands the polarities of energy and what they can do
- Increases your awareness of synchronicity
- Helps you understand potential dangers

Meaning in Divination: Isa is the polar opposite of the first rune, Fehu, the primal fire that began creation. The positive side of Isa is that there are times when stasis can be helpful in assimilating information-particularly when a lot of input is directed your way, and you need time to evaluate it. The negative qualities of Isa are stagnation and procrastination. When they take over, the energy around you feels frozen in place, and it needs to start moving again.

Isa symbolizes the force of attraction, gravity, inertia, and entropy in Oneness. Because of this centralizing and concentrating effect, it represents the individual ego, the energy that holds the ego and self together during stressful times. It is the place where the past and the future come together, molding the present into form.

✱malachite✱

Element: Earth
Color: Green
Numerological Value: 12
Astrology: The Sun
Tarot Card: The Emperor

JERA (yar-awe)

Tree: Oak

Gemstones: Emerald, malachite, adverturine, green tourmaline

Key Words: Cycles, right action, completion, fertility, natural law, continuation

Mythology: Jera represents time as a whole and is also the god of sunshine. The world emerges from the ice of the third rune Isa, into the fire of Jera, much as the seasons move from winter to spring every year.

Magical Qualities:

 * Understands the circular flow of Oneness
 * Works with natural patterns, such as seasonal cycles
 * Increases creativity and fertility
 * Increases harmony
 * Learns how polarities work together to make the whole
 * Harnesses the power of manifestation

Meaning in Divination: Jera embodies dynamic form, change toward completion. One of the two "central runes" in the scheme of the Elder Futhark, Jera affirms the cyclical nature of this world, including the twelve-fold cycle of the Sun. It deals with the Sun's yearly path, as Raidho deals with the Sun's daily path and guiding force.

With its relation to the annual cycle, Jera symbolizes natural law and the fruitfulness of effort. If your meditation practice upon this rune is set up in accordance with natural laws, and the energy is with you, your spiritual harvest will be abundant.

EIHWAZ (eye-waz)

Element: **All the elements**
Color: **Dark blue**
Numerological Value: **13**
Astrology: **Scorpio**
Tarot Card: **The Hanged Man**
Tree: **Yew**
Gemstones: **Lapis lazuli, sapphire, blue topaz, herkimer diamond**
Key Words: **Communication, death, regeneration, knowledge, dreaming, magic**
Mythology: **Eihwaz is associated with Odin's discovery of the runes and their meanings, as well as with his ability to travel between the realms of life and death. Eihwaz is also associated with Uller, god of hunting and archery.**

Magical Qualities:

* Understands the knowledge of the cosmic or World Tree
* Releases you from the fear of death
* Develops your creative and magical abilities
* Increases your divination skills
* Communicates between different realms of awareness
* Practices lucid dreaming
* Communicates with your ancestors

Meaning in Divination: As the axis that connects the three realms of the upperworld and the underworld, Eihwaz is a life-giving energy and a powerful stave of protection and banishing. With Eihwaz, the emphasis is on communication and the connections between the three realms-in other words, moving through the thresholds.

Eihwaz is ideal for working with different planes of being, including the realm of dreams. When you use this rune as a meditation tool, it may reveal a new or different stage or course in life. It can also be used for protection and to move someone's energy out of your space. Keep in mind that the number thirteen is the most powerful magical number; it only began to be considered unlucky with the advent of Christianity.

PERDHRO (perth-row)

Element: Water
Color: Black or silver
Numerological Value: 14
Astrology: Saturn
Tarot Card: The Wheel of Fortune
Tree: Beech
Gemstones: Moonstone, obsidian, clear quartz
Key Words: Birth, wisdom, kinship, manifestation, chance, luck
Mythology: The three Norns together, are in charge of

Perdhro. The Norns control the powers of cause and effect. The Norns also control time, since the cause and effect sequence takes place through time, and the past overlaps into the future to bring about present reality.

Magical Qualities:
* Perceives your fate-past, future, and present
* Understands the nature of cause and effect
* Taps into infinite Oneness
* Seeks the wisdom to make things work for you
* Understands the power of future sight
* Knows where your patterns are going to lead

Meaning in Divination: Perdhro symbolizes the energy that controls your fate. Underlying this are the laws of cause and effect or action and reaction.

By becoming aware of the synchronicity in your life, you can evolve and become more knowledgeable about the energies that move, influence, and propel you forward. The perception of Perdhro is a paradox-constant change that always remains the same. Once again, it is the polarities of energy that give this rune meaning.

The rune of time and duration, Perdhro can help bring all your goals and aspirations to fruition. Perdhro embodies the great pattern, containing the potential for cosmic manifestation.

It is also the rune of balance maintained within Oneness.

Whenever this balance is altered, energy is displaced, and it then moves again to balance itself. In your meditation practice, make an effort to become aware of the consequences of your life patterns so that they come out the way you intend. Work with the energy of Perdhro to gain wisdom and divination ability. As a vessel, the Perdhro rune holds the energy of the runes as a whole.

ALGIZ (all-geese)

Element: Air
Color: Rainbow
Numerological Value: 15
Astrology: Cancer
Tarot Card: The Moon
Tree: Yew
Gemstones: Rainbow tourmaline, fluorite, agate, jasper, diamond
Key Words: Spirit, protection, sanctuary, refuge, power, divinity
Mythology: Algiz is depicted as the god Tyr's hand that he sacrificed to keep away the embodiment of the powers of chaos and darkness that were to end the world. As one of the oldest rune symbols, Algiz represents the three faces of the gods and goddesses, as well as the three polarities of energy: positive, neutral, and negative. Other mythological references to the number three include the runes themselves, which are divided into the three aettir, and the three realms

of existence: upper, middle, and lower. Algiz is the embodiment of the human spirit as it strives toward Divinity.

Magical Qualities:
- ✳ Protects and defends from harm
- ✳ Moves toward the completion of your patterns
- ✳ Taps into the Divine three-fold and nine-fold patterns
- ✳ Understands your Divine connection
- ✳ Communes with the elements
- ✳ Increases your regenerative powers

Meaning in Divination: Algiz is a primary rune of protection. Along with Thurisaz, the Algiz rune provides a line of defense guaranteed to stop-or at least slow down-any invader. In an energetic sense, "invader" means anyone you don't want in your physical or energetic space.

Along with protection, the energy of Algiz represents the movement upward toward the divine from which we originated. In terms of meditation, it means having your energetic patterns take flight and move toward a successful outcome.

Turned on its side, Algiz looks like a flying swan or goose. The polarity involves protecting yourself while you are in those initial stages of flight, before you master your wings. If you feel yourself being attacked energetically, visualize the Algiz rune standing protectively around you on all sides, above, and below. Then focus on your energetic patterns coming to fruition.

SOWILO (so-wheel-o)

Element: Fire

Color: Gold

Numerological Value: 16

Astrology: The Sun

Tarot Card: The Sun

Tree: Juniper

Gemstones: Ruby, carnelian, citrine, golden topaz, red cat's-eye

Key Words: Partnership, journey, power, transformation, understanding

Mythology: Sowilo is associated with the Sun and the contrast and polarity between light and dark times of the year— a universal force in agricultural and nature-driven cultures.

Magical Qualities:
* Illuminates and fuels your magical patterns
* Develops your psychic abilities
* Is aware of your relationships with other people
* Moves in the direction of enlightenment
* Expands your awareness of the solar cycles
* Helps your patterns come to fruition

Meaning in Divination: Sowilo represents the energy that brings you full circle to fruition. While Raidho represents the circular pattern itself, Sowilo symbolizes the fuel that propels it. Ultimately, all patterns have a circular or spiral nature.

Straight lines never truly exist, because in space all lines eventually curve and feed back into themselves, becoming a circle; thus the fruition and, in turn, the destruction of all patterns.

Much like Wunjo at the end of the first aett, Sowilo is the culmination of the lessons contained in the second aett. It is the coming to fruition of your efforts, whether positive or negative. When your patterns and goals progress in a positive way, they lift you to the next level, the third aett. But if you fail to build a good foundation, everything may come toppling down around you. Each aett is a building block to the next, just as each rune moves you to the next. From one rune to the next, you progress.

The Third Aett

TIWAZ (tea-was)

Element: Air

Color: Bright red

Numerological Value: 17

Astrology: Libra

Tarot Card: Justice

Tree: Oak

Gemstones: Ruby, garnet, jasper, bloodstone, golden topaz, citrine

Key Words: Justice, order, victory, support, self-sacrifice, faith, loyalty

Mythology: Tiwaz is the rune of the god of heaven, Tyr, and the god of mystery, Mithra. Tyr is also the god of sacrifice, patron of warriors, making Tiwaz the rune of warriors, spiritual warriors in particular. Traditionally, warriors scratched Tiwaz on their spear tips and on the hilts of their swords.

Magical Qualities:
* Increases your faith in the universe
* Evaluates and judges what needs to be done
* Obtains the successful completion of patterns
* Builds your spiritual energy

* Develops your personal spirituality
* Teaches how to use order to your benefit

Meaning in Divination: Tiwaz embodies the mystery of spirituality and faith, according to the Divine patterns of Oneness. Representing the male polarity, Tiwaz energy is characterized as being warlike and aggressive. On one side, it represents law and justice, but on the other side it embodies an unemotional energy that can be stern and not very nurturing. This rune energizes defense and outward expansion, in that male energy seeks to defend what it has, while at the same time aggressively pursuing what it doesn't have yet. Meditate upon the Tiwaz rune to move your goals forward, particularly when there seems to be a struggle among the energies present.

BERKANA (bur-kan-a)

Element: Earth
Color: Dark green
Numerological Value: 18
Astrology: Virgo
Tarot Card: The Empress
Tree: Birch
Gemstones: All gemstones

Key Words: Nurturing, rebirth, growth, transition, spirit, concealment, protection, ancestry
Mythology: Birch trees are consecrated to the god Thor, and symbolize nurturing and the return of spring.

Magical Qualities:

* Works with the feminine energies
* Understands the forces of transition
* Conceals and protects energy
* Revitalizes the spirit and personal empowerment
* Gathers and directs the powers of Earth, Air, and Water
* Increases intuitive ability
* Perfects magical skills

Meaning in Divination: Berkana's intrinsic quality revolves around the life, death, and rebirth triad, which brings with it transition. As Mother Goddess, Berkana brings life and is the mother of all manifestation, representing the energies of birth and rebirth on a cosmic, as well as a human, level. Berkana also embodies the dark aspect of the Mother Goddess-the opposite polarity-death. Here, it symbolizes the death of the old self and rebirth, or transition, into the new. So, Berkana rules over the four transitory stages: birth, adolescence, marriage, and death.

The Berkana rune is therefore the rune of becoming, of fulfilling your potential, and evolving on a spiritual level. It may signify new beginnings or the end of a cycle. Meditate upon Berkana for laying foundations, and then cultivating them with the nurturing care of the Earth, Air, and Water goddess.

EHWAZ (ee-waz)

Element: Earth

Color: White

Numerological Value: 19

Astrology: Gemini

Tarot Card: The Lovers

Tree: Oak/Ash

Gemstones: Milky quartz, diamond, clear quartz,
pearl, amber

Key Words: Duality, movement, partnership,
interaction, harmony

Mythology: Ehwaz is associated with Odin's horse, Sleipnir,
product of a god Loki and another powerful stallion.

Magical Qualities:

* Enhances magical power and wisdom
* Travels to other realms and dimensions of being
* Encourages lucid dreaming ability
* Increases the swiftness of your personal patterns
* Works with polarities of energy
* Understands the harmony in relationships
* Shape-shifts and works with your power animals
* Projects the double

Meaning in Divination: This rune represents a journey in consciousness that is protected, supported, or guided. The
emphasis here is on partnerships and working together, and

often denotes assistance from another person or energetic helper, such as a "fetch" (a spirit double).

Ehwaz relates to partnerships and joint ventures of all types. It can unify two people in a strong, harmonious relationship, either on a personal or a business level. Ehwaz is a great rune for marriage meditation, because it emphasizes cooperative interaction between people. Because of its connection with traveling between different realms, Ehwaz represents the astral or energetic body-the part of your being that can be projected outside your physical body. Ehwaz denotes dream power and astral travel.

MANNAZ (man-nawz)

Element: Air
Color: Rainbow
Numerological Value: 20
Astrology: Jupiter
Tarot Card: The Magician
Tree: Holly
Gemstones: Bloodstone, ruby, garnet, amber, rainbow tourmaline, smithsonite, amethyst
Key Words: Godhood and goddesshood, memory, humanity, order, intelligence, ancestors, sacred union
Mythology: Mannaz represents the evolving human intelligence. It is the symbol of the god Heimdall, the genetic link between the gods and goddesses and humankind and the

being who brings forth the three levels of social structure: the provider, the warrior, and the priest-king.

Magical Qualities:
  * Increases mental powers such as knowledge, memory, and wisdom
    * Perceives the Divine and human nature in yourself and others
    * Works with the social order to perpetuate your patterns
    * Understands the polarities of personality
    * Accesses ancestral memory
    * Understands the concept of incarnation

Meaning in Divination: In its perfect state, Mannaz symbolizes the complete human being, one who integrates the wisdom of the runes with the self. This rune is associated with perfection and the conscious application of the individual's will. It embodies the idea of this will being directed toward the common good of an entire group.

People are the main influence and focus in the Mannaz rune. It stands for the social order and shows how through this order you can achieve your full potential on a human and Divine level of being. Understanding this order is essential to creating positive and successful life patterns.

LAGUZ (la-gooz)

Element: Water

Color: Deep blue-green

Numerological Value: 21

Astrology: Waxing Moon

Tarot Card: The Star

Tree: Willow

Gemstones: Aquamarine, azurite, calcite, chrysocolla, fluorite

Key Words: Fluidity, life force, birth

Mythology: Laguz represents the source from which all rivers of energy flow into the ocean, which in this case is Oneness. In its Old Norse form of "logr," meaning sorcery, this rune relates to the goddess Freyja, who introduced the practice of magic to the Aesir. In particular she taught Odin seidr, a type of love magic that had previously been practiced only by women.

Magical Qualities:

* Increases your living spark by your becoming aware of it
* Tunes into the watery flow of life
* Becomes familiar with the energies of life and death
* Increases the flow of your personal patterns
* Understands and integrates your emotions and desires
* Immerses you in Divine Knowledge
* Washes away negative energies and unwanted patterns

Meaning in Divination: Symbolic of the seed as it meets water and begins the life process, Laguz is a symbol of the expansion of life in both physical and spiritual realms, and the planting of energetic patterns that sprout quickly from the Earth.

Also connected to this concept are the tides, which energetically move inward and outward, rising and ebbing on a daily basis. The tides reflect energy's natural flow in an up-and-down, back-and-forth motion that is universal. It is important to remember that, when you practice meditation, you need to account for this ebb and flow of energy as it moves back and forth between negative and positive poles. The idea is to accentuate the positive flow while minimizing the negative.

INGWAZ *(ing-was)*

Element: Earth
Color: Yellow
Numerological Value: 22
Astrology: The dark Moon
Tarot Card: Judgment
Tree: Apple
Gemstones: Malachite, rose quartz, citrine, golden topaz, adventurine, amber, chrysoprase
Key Words: Energy, gestation, integration, male fertility, protection, castration
Mythology: Ingwaz is the old German Earth god of male fertility, the house hearth, and the inglenook (a nook by a large, open

fireplace). The rune symbolizes the protection of house-holds. This rune is also related to the experience of women who deal with the mystery of fecundity and birth.

Magical Qualities:
- ✱ Useful as a sacred enclosure for magic
- ✱ Learns the nature of diverse energies
- ✱ Understands the forces of change that bring initiation and transition
- ✱ Understands fertility in terms of complete patterns
- ✱ Learns to channel energies into a single, focused intent
- ✱ Understands love and sex magic

Meaning in Divination: Although powerful, Ingwaz does not release energy immediately, but instead builds it up and releases it in a single burst. The more energy you have to channel, the greater the thrust of energy toward that intention. The more energy you move toward an outcome, the more likely the outcome will be realized, which is why this rune is associated with fertility.

DAGAZ *(da-gauze or thaw-gauze)*

Element: Fire

Color: Blue

Numerological Value: 23

Astrology: The waxing and
waning Moon

Tarot Card: Temperance

Tree: Spruce

Gemstones: Lapis lazuli, sodalite, amazonite,
azurite, blue zircon, sapphire

Key Words: Light, enlightenment, polarity,
awakening, intuition, well-being

Mythology: Dagaz relates to a dark-light polarity, associated with
dark dwarfs and white (or light) elves. Gentle and kind, as light
as air itself, and with no ill will or greed, the elves possessed
supernatural powers and were considered Divine helpers.

Magical Qualities:

* Understands the powers of darkness and light
* Uses the Sun's fire to fuel magical patterns
* Knows how to move through the dark without fear
* Merges with the cycle of light
* Provides spiritual enlightenment

Meaning in Divination: Dagaz refers to that shamanic state in
which polarities of energy come together:"the razor's edge."

This may be a time of enlightenment and awakening, not only harnessing the powerful fire energy that gets things done, but the wisdom to best use the energies. Fire energy can get things done or burn things up. When used with wisdom, it can help your plans come to fruition, in much the same way that the Sun provides the sustenance that sustains all life. Meditating on the Dagaz rune can help you energize yourself so that your life can become more fruitful.

OTHALA (oath-awe-la)

Element: Air, mastery of all elements
Color: Deep yellow
Numerological Value: 24
Astrology: The Full Moon
Tarot Card: The Moon
Tree: Hawthorn
Gemstones: Diamond, emerald, ruby, clear quartz, amber
Key Words: Ancestry, prosperity, inheritance, DNA, family
Mythology: The oldest literal meaning of Othala is "noble" or "prince." Odin is the god of Othala, questing for all wisdom and the possibility of everlasting immortality. Understanding the polarities of Oneness-the powers of life and death-brings us to that point when all the elements of Oneness are reconciled and balanced. If you have the power to endure, to aim for divinity, then action follows thought and you reach your intention and actualize your dreams.

Magical Qualities:

- ✲ Understands the implications of the whole
- ✲ Comprehends the wisdom and integration of all things
- ✲ Uses the lessons of the past to better deal with the future
- ✲ Is at one with the source of everything
- ✲ Works with the elements of the sacred land
- ✲ Communicates with the sleepers
- ✲ Achieves goddesshood or godhood
- ✲ Increases your lucid dreaming ability

Meaning in Divination: Othala is the rune of Oneness. When you experience Oneness, you have wisdom about everything that was, will be, and is, your desires manifest according to your intention, and you become wise like Odin.

Othala may represent everything coming to divine fruition or, at the other pole, being completely destroyed. It is all or nothing as the third aett closes. If you travel wisely through the runic stream, you become one with everything and become a Divine Being. All paths try to lead you to the Divine state of affinity with Oneness, at which level anything is possible.

Meditations

Twenty-Four-Week Rune Meditation

This meditation takes a twenty-four-week commitment, but the results are guaranteed to expand your mind and your knowledge of the runes. Ideally, begin this meditation on Wednesday. Use a rune stone, card, or square for this meditation, so that you have a physical point of reference.

1. The first week (Wednesday through Tuesday), you will focus on Fehu; the second week, Uruz; the third week, Thurisaz; and so on, for twenty-four weeks, moving through one of the three aettir every eight weeks. After selecting the rune of the week, read over the rune description in this book.

2. Notice how the rune and its primary energies influence your life during the week. Make notes as to how you feel about the weekly rune, and record some of your thoughts about the process. You may find that the rune will have a much stronger and more active influence when you work with it after doing this meditation.

3. The following is very basic guideline for helping you focus on each of the aettir and the twenty-four runes. For instance, week one, concentrate on mobile wealth–where you find yourself financially, where you would like to find yourself financially, and how the Fehu rune can strengthen your personal wealth.

1st Aett—The Aett of Creation.

1. Fehu-Financial prosperity and mobile wealth

2. Uruz-Health and healing issues

3. Thurisaz-Conflicts, obstacles, and psychological issues

4. Ansuz-Communications and transmissions; points things back to sources in the past

5. Raidho-The direction of your personal path

6. Kenaz-New ways of experiencing things, new opportunities, information, and creativity

7. Gebo-Issues having to do with an exchange of energies such as contracts, gifts, relationships, and partnerships

8. Wunjo-Your wishes, hopes, achievements, and accomplishments

2nd Aett—The Aett of Humanity.

9. Hagalaz-Issues of change and transformation, sometimes disruptive, but often for the better

10. Naudhiz-Anything that restricts you, or situations that make you anxious or fearful

11. Isa-All of those things you have trouble letting go of, especially past hurts and pain, things that have crystallized; this is the rune of your conditioning

12. Jera-Your hopes and expectations, and the harvest rune that shows the results of your actions and efforts

13. Eihwaz-The driving force of motivation and your sense of purpose

14. Perdhro-Your hidden talents, intuitive abilities, and creative powers

15. Algiz-Your protective powers and spiritual connections with the divine

16. Sowilo-Your sunshine in life and the direction in which you will be guided by Divine Light

3rd Aett—The Aett of Divinity or Godhood.

17. Tiwaz-Your personal strengths, initiative, honor, sense of justice and fair play, and leadership abilities

18. Berkana-Your feminine power and intuitions; issues with family and personal growth

19. Ehwaz-Your abilities of cooperation, sexual expression, and relationships with others

20. Mannaz-Your social position and the people around you, including your friends and enemies

21. Laguz-Your emotions and powers of imagination

22. Ingwaz-The way you integrate your life; your expectations

23. Dagaz-Your balance between polarities; issues of initiation, birth, and new beginnings

24. Othala-Your spiritual heritage and birthright

Sensing the Runes

This simple meditation takes only about five minutes a day and produces excellent results. It's a good idea to apply this meditation to each of the twenty-four Elder Futhark over an extended period of time.

1. Sit in a place where you will not be disturbed and, if possible, set a timer for five minutes. Select your favorite rune and place it facing up in front of you. Take a few deep breaths, relax your mind and body, and make any adjustments needed to get comfortable.

2. Begin looking at the rune in front of you, perceiving it with all your senses, including your intuition and psychic ability. Use your imagination. See, touch, taste, smell, and hear the rune. Be in the moment with the rune. If you feel yourself wavering and moving away from the experience, go back to the rune and again experience it with all your senses.

3. Any time your mind tries to take over the experience, move back to the rune and sense it with another one of your senses. Do this for five minutes at a time. As you practice this technique, you will become better at staying in the moment with the rune and its essential energies.

Rune Awareness

Take at least fifteen minutes to do this meditation. When you finish, select one rune to work with for the day and put the remainder away in your rune bag or box.

1. Place the twenty-four Elder Futhark runes, in the form of rune stones, squares, or cards, face-up in front of you. Arrange them in their three aettir (sets of eight), yet space them out so you can look at each one individually.

2. Sit or stand comfortably. Clear your mind, let go of distracting thoughts, and take a few deep breaths, inhaling to the count of six and exhaling to the count of six.

3. One at a time, look at the runes, making a mental note of how your perception moves as you see the runes in front of you. Allow your awareness to drift slowly from symbol to symbol, focusing for a few moments on each one. Be particularly aware of your intellectual process and how it works in relation to the symbols you are studying. Do you dissect the symbols, one by one, analyzing their essential elements? Do certain runes evoke sensations or memories, which then connect to other sensations and memories?

4. Think how each runic symbol relates to your present life, noticing how some seem to resonate with you more than others. As you focus on each symbol, chant the name of the rune over and over. Notice what effect this has on your perception and any related body sensations.

One Rune a Day
Select one rune each day, for twenty-four days.

1. Upon waking, mix your runes stones, squares, or cards in a bag or box, and with intention, but without looking, pull the one that you feel most drawn to. Draw the rune symbol on several scraps of paper or sticky notes and carry or place them so that you will see the symbol continually throughout the day.

2. You will begin to feel the chosen runes resonate inside you. Sometimes the rune seems to correspond to a part of your body, or you may find that you see the rune symbol wherever you look-in road signs, the shapes of trees, the way pencils fall together on a desk, and so forth.

3. For these twenty-four days, record the rune you pull each day on a sheet of paper. Go back and look at the sheet and notice how many times certain runes were pulled during the twenty-four-day period, and which runes were not pulled. The runes that appear most often reflect the influences that are currently the strongest in your daily life. The runes not pulled reflect energies that are not yet directly influencing your life.

Index